THE LEAP

The Science of Trust and Why It Matters

Ulrich Boser

New Harvest
Houghton Mifflin Harcourt
BOSTON   NEW YORK
2014

This edition published by special arrangement with Amazon Publishing

For information about permission to reproduce selections
from this book, go to www.apub.com.

www.hmhco.com

Library of Congress Cataloging-in-Publication Data
Boser, Ulrich.
The leap : the science of trust and why it matters / Ulrich Boser.
pages cm.
Includes bibliographical references.
ISBN 978-0-544-26201-0 (hardcover)
1. Trust. I. Title.
BF575.T7B67 2014
302'.1—dc23
2013045584

Printed in the United States of America
DOC 10 9 8 7 6 5 4 3 2 1

To those who have trusted me

Contents

Author's Note   vii

Introduction   ix

PART I: WHY WE TRUST

1. The Social Instinct: Why We Trust   3

2. Reciprocity, Indirect Reciprocity, and What We Can Learn from Hector Ramirez   19

3. How We Trust: The Lessons of Clark Rockefeller   34

4. Can We Trust Again?: Learning from Rwanda   47

PART II: HOW WE CAN IMPROVE TRUST

5. Teams: "Go on Faith and Knowledge"   73

6. The Economy: The Art of Trustworthiness   80

7. Government: Trusting the Tax Man   89

8. Politics: "Encourage You to Be Nasty"   102

9. Technology: Communication, Community, and Couchsurfing   115

10. Path Forward: Sometimes We Need to Leap   125

Acknowledgments   133

The State of Trust   137

Tool Kit for Policymakers   139

Notes   141

Author's Note

Please connect with me on Facebook or Twitter or email me at ulrich@ulrichboser.com. I will also keep a running log of errors, clarifications, and questions on my website, ulrichboser.com.

While this is an original work of nonfiction, I have relied on many outside sources for quotes, data, and other factual information, which I have cited in the endnotes. In some instances, I have used text that first appeared in other publications. That is also indicated in the endnotes. If a quote is in italics, it means that the words may not be exact. In some instances, I may have altered quotes for grammar and clarity.

To ensure accuracy, I shared some portions of the book with experts or sources. I also hired a fact-checker to help vet the accuracy of the material. All errors of logic, fact, or writing are, no doubt, mine.

Introduction

Most of the members of the Old Christians rugby team slept in. It was the morning of October 13, 1972, and some bad weather had grounded the rugby team's charter flight to Santiago, Chile. Some of the young men had been out dancing the night before, and when they finally straggled into the airport later that day, the rugby players taunted the airplane pilots: Were the pilots too scared to cross the mountains?

The Fairchild finally rose into the sky in the early afternoon while some of the team members played card games.[1] A few tossed a rugby football down the aisle, yelling "Think fast!"[2] When a spot of turbulence shook the plane, they whooped like bullfighters.

As the small plane flew over a narrow, mountainous pass, it slipped into a dense bank of clouds. Strong winds started to rattle the aircraft. At one point, the turboprop dropped a few hundred feet, and when the clouds finally drew apart again, a rocky cliff appeared just beyond one of the wings.

"Is it normal to fly so close to the mountains?" one of the passengers asked.[3]

"I don't think so," his friend answered.

Moments later, there was a long shudder. A rocky crag scraped the bottom of the fuselage, and the tail section crashed away. The wings broke off. The plane soared for a moment or two before skidding down the slope of a mountain, and among the lifeless bodies and splintered luggage, there were more than two dozen survivors who spent the night huddled in the broken plane.[4]

The cold was severe, something profound, and the group didn't have any warm coats. The team had packed for a trip to the ocean, not the mountains. Even worse, there was no food. The men had just a few candies and a bit of dried fruit, and within days the survivors began to feed on the frozen corpses scattered around the crash site. Sometimes the meat was cooked. Usually it was eaten raw. Then, roughly two weeks after the crash, a blanket of wet snow killed another half dozen men. "It is hard to describe the depths of the despair that fell upon us in the wake of the avalanche," writes Nando Parrado in his memoir, *Miracle in the Andes*. "Now we saw that we would never be safe in this place."

Among the men, the urge to be selfish, to take a little more food or clothing or water for themselves, was strong. Everyone was deeply hungry. Everyone was exquisitely cold. Yet the survivors figured out a way to come together, as documentaries like *Stranded* have suggested. They created a strict system for sleeping positions, since spots farther away from the door were warmer and more comfortable.[5] Everyone received the exact same ration of cigarettes.[6] The men continued to care for the wounded, massaging the feet of the injured to save their toes from frostbite.[7] "When one suffered, everyone did. If someone did something wrong, everyone reacted," Fito Strauch told the producers of *Stranded*.[8] "There was no room for anyone to do anything that was against the general interest. It was like a nineteen-bodied organism."

Nearly two months after the crash, two of the survivors managed to trek out of the mountains, and the Chilean Air Force eventually saved the rest of the group. In the years since the dramatic rescue, the story of the crash has become the subject of movies, books, and documentaries, and the attraction is clear: People want to know how the group made it out alive. There are some obvious reasons for their survival. Many of the men were athletes, strong and well trained. The survivors were also young and determined. They wanted to return home, to see their families, to see their friends. Religion also played a role, and many of the survivors saw the eating of the dead bodies as something almost holy.

Perhaps most remarkable, though, is that the men built up a sense of faith in each other. Or, as Nando Parrado writes in *Miracle in the*

Andes, "None of us were saints. We survived not because we were per-fect, but because the accumulated weight of our concern for each other far outweighed our natural self-interest."

Today, many of the survivors are in their sixties. They're doctors, lawyers, and architects. They own houses. They have grandchildren. For three decades now, the group has gotten together every Decem-ber to celebrate their survival. In those moments, it seems, the men renew the community that they once created, a community built on the promise that they made to each other while they were starving in the Andes: If one of them died, the others could eat his body so that they could live.

According to popular wisdom, what happened in the Andes should not have happened. No one stuck in subzero temperatures is supposed to give up his blanket. No one stranded in a crashed airplane is sup-posed to share his sweater with someone else, and today, almost 60 percent of Americans argue that you "can't be too careful in dealing with people."[9] Just about one in ten Americans thinks that their busi-ness leaders are honest.[10] In my own research, I've found that in some states almost no one says that they fully trust other people.

The conventional wisdom isn't fully accurate, though, and our sense of faith can be restored. We can improve our social bonds, and the reason is simple, as researcher Pamela Paxton once pointed out.[11] Our deeply negative view of others doesn't match up with the science, and it turns out that we evolved to work with others. We have a deep-seated urge to be fair and warmhearted.[12] The headlines might suggest a nation filled with greedy jerks and selfish egoists, with scam artists and Ponzi schemes, but our raw impulsive response is often to place our faith in others and return that faith once it's given.[13]

What's more, trust turns out to be a type of "social glue," and our faith in others builds social capital.[14] It creates social networks. It's what keeps every group together, whether it's a team of football play-ers or a nation of hundreds of millions. Or think back to the men in the Andes. If they didn't have some sort of faith in each other, they could never have lived for seventy-two days in one of the world's most desolate places.

My goal with this book is to better understand our faith in others and provide some ways to improve social trust. Or, to paraphrase Nando Parrado, I want to show how we can make our concern for each other outweigh our natural self-interest. Before we go any further, though, we have to acknowledge that society has changed, and we will not return to the social cohesion of the 1950s anytime soon. Some form of individualism is here to stay. But, at the same time, we all need to be part of something bigger than ourselves. We're all motivated by more than our own self-interest, and greater levels of social cohesion can dramatically improve the nation's well-being. It can boost health outcomes — and jump-start the economy. As we'll see, social trust can even drive down the nation's murder rate.

I decided to write this book after working on an initiative to improve faith in government for the Center for American Progress, a nonpartisan think tank where I'm a fellow. I became fascinated with the new research on why we trust others. I soon began visiting psychology research labs. Obscure economic studies became my bedtime reading. Neuroscientist Brooks King-Casas once scanned my brain in an fMRI to help me better understand the neuroscience of cooperation.

In other words, this book builds upon the work of many others. I'm indebted in particular to the research and writings of Yochai Benkler, Bruce Schneier, and Robert Putnam.[15] An essay by Jeremy Adam Smith and Pamela Paxton titled "America's Trust Fall" was an early and important inspiration.[16] But I might be most grateful for the help of Paul Zak, a neuroeconomist at Claremont Graduate University. Zak and I went skydiving together to see if the experience would increase my levels of oxytocin, the so-called trust hormone, and I'm deeply appreciative of any source that is willing to roar through the heavens with me at 120 miles per hour.

In this book, I examine the degree to which we broadly trust others, or what researchers call *social trust*. I rely on a well-cited definition of our faith in others, which I've paraphrased here: Trust is when you assume vulnerability with an optimistic expectation of someone else.[17] This sort of trust comes in different forms. There's what experts call *calculation-based trust,* where we place our faith in someone by estimating the chance that they might betray us.[18] This sort of trust is logical, a type of risk. But it often turns into what's called *relational trust,* which is more emotional, less rational, and when it comes to relational trust, we often want some sort of connection. The other thing to keep in mind is that the study of trust remains young, and like many things that are young, there is uncertainty. And so while the ideas contained in this book are rooted in the latest thinking, not everything is conclusive.

With regard to the narrative, the first part of the book is devoted to understanding the basics of trust. I'll discuss oxytocin and describe how with a single dose of this chemical, people become more trusting. I'll also look at how and why we place our faith in strangers and discuss the role that our everyday experiences play in our faith in others. Throughout the book, I'll focus on some of the key drivers of trust, from social networks to a sense of empowerment. I'll also look at the crucial roles of culture and government and social capital. I also hope to underscore the role of trustworthiness, because without dependability, without honesty and transparency, trust can't exist.

In the second half of the book, we'll look at some ways that we can use our knowledge of trust to improve the world we live in. I'll look at how we can increase trust in teams and how technology is changing our sense of faith in others, and we'll find out, for instance, how a website helped a young military cadet and a middle-aged, gay nudist become friends. I'll also talk about some of the ways we might boost trust in government, which can go a long way to support our faith in others. Americans currently have a better opinion of cockroaches than they do of Congress, and we will look at why that matters — and what we can do about it.[19]

As part of my research, I traveled to Rwanda to better understand how the African nation is rebuilding a sense of trust. In the back of the book, I've included a policy tool kit that outlines what our government can do to restore our faith in others. Ultimately, I hope to convince you that we can recover our feeling of connection, our sense of community, and through the power of our trusting ways, through the strength of our social nature, we can build a more meaningful society.

But for now, let's start with a different leap of faith. Let's start with a game known as Split or Steal.

PART I

Why We Trust

Chapter 1

_____

The Social Instinct

Why We Trust

T HE British TV program *Golden Balls* was a standard afternoon
game show. There was a sappy host, a glittery stage, and lots
of flashing lights.[1] The show had a strong run with some two
million viewers in the late 2000s, and the contestants came from a
variety of backgrounds. One worked as an accounts manager. Another
as a medical secretary. Some were young men. Others were middle-
aged women. All of them dreamed of taking home the show's jackpot,
which could be as much as $175,000.

The show itself was a mash-up of *Deal or No Deal* and *Survivor.* In
the last round, the two most successful contestants would sit in the
middle of the brightly lit stage and compete face-to-face in a game
called Split or Steal. The basic premise of Split or Steal was this: If the
players worked together, they would share the jackpot. If one player
cooperated and the other player betrayed, the double-crosser would
keep the jackpot for himself. The twist was that if both players double-
crossed each other, then neither of them would get anything. Or, as the
show's host would say to the players in a deep voice: *You go home with
nothing.*

To get a flavor of the game, imagine for a moment that you're playing Split or Steal for a jackpot of $100,000.[2] The overhead lights are

hot and bright. Your hands shake with anxiety. Everything seems loud, almost neon, and so you take some time to mull your options.

If you work with your partner, if you cooperate with him or her, you might take home $50,000. That's a lot of money. More than enough for a new car.

And yet you have no idea if your partner will work with you. After all, your partner is also probably dreaming of a better car, and there's nothing holding your partner back from double-crossing you. There are no laws against being nasty to someone else on a television game show. Put simply, there doesn't seem to be any good reason to trust your partner.

What's more, if you betray your partner and manage to double-cross him or her, you will take home $100,000, and with that sort of money, you could make a down payment on an oceanside condo in Florida.

In a way, the research questions posed by Split or Steal are obvious: In a real-world test of trust and cooperation, do individuals show any faith in strangers? If hundreds of thousands of dollars are on the line, do most people do the right thing?

A few years ago, two economists, Donja Darai and Silvia Grätz, tried to answer these questions, and what they found was surprising. It turned out that most of the people who played Split or Steal trusted the other. Despite the fact that that the logical thing to do in the game was to betray the other person, more than 50 percent of the contestants showed a sense of faith in their partner.

What's more, one of the best predictors of whether or not the players worked together was the degree to which they had some sort of meaningful interaction. If the two people talked about cooperating, if they made a clear and concrete promise to help each other, they were far more likely to trust. In fact, a conversation between the two players remained a powerful predictor of cooperation even after considering factors like gender, where the individuals grew up, and even their previous history of betraying others. The only thing that made the bond between the players stronger? If they shook hands or hugged each other. In other words, the only factor that made a verbal connection stronger was underscoring it with a physical connection.

If you read a lot of blogs, if you watch a lot of YouTube, if you pay attention to game show hosts, you might believe that you're never supposed to put your faith in a stranger. After all, people are not supposed to be trustworthy. This notion is widespread, and social trust is the lowest it has been in decades. Survey after survey shows weak levels of social cohesion, and selfishness has become central to all sorts of ideas and beliefs, from psychology to business. Or take the Split or Steal study. When I reached out to Donja Darai in her offices at the University of Zurich, she told me that many experts believe "that people are only interested in maximizing their own profit." But, she added, "That's clearly not the whole story."

In fact, that's far from the whole story, and it turns out that we innately care about others. We're wired to live in groups, and for many of us, trust and trustworthiness are unconscious, automatic, a part of our habitual brains. And in most experiments that measure trust and trustworthiness, individuals will invest half of their cash in a stranger, and many people are reliable and give some money back.[3] In another series of studies involving American college students, neuroeconomist Paul Zak has found that as many as 90 percent of subjects trusted people that they didn't know and around 95 percent of those subjects were trustworthy.[4]

The results of these sorts of trust experiments suggest that our faith in others is a part of "human nature," as economist Kay-Yut Chen argues. The research also indicates that our tendency to trust — and be trustworthy — will shift depending on the situation, and if people play a Split or Steal–type game against a real person, they trust more than if they play against a computer. But perhaps the most striking conclusion is regarding the role of human bonds, and our social ties, our notions of togetherness, the network of relationships that make up our daily lives: They all support our sense of trust. We see this in the Split or Steal study, where people who shared social connections were more likely to trust each other. We see this in other trust experiments, too. When psychologists recently played a version of the Split or Steal game with adults who had been brought up in single-child households in China, they found those people to be less trusting than the people who grew up with siblings. China's one-child policy "has given rise to a land of 'little emperors' whose parents dote on them exclusively," the authors concluded.[5]

Our deeply cooperative nature might offer the best way to restore our sense of social trust, as Smith and Paxton suggest. But before we examine that idea, we should gain a better sense of just how social we are as a species, and consider for a moment what happens to people who are placed in solitary confinement. For many of us, a few months by oneself in a room might not seem like a terrible punishment. Sure, you'll miss your friends and family. You'll be bored and irritated and maybe a bit lonely. But if you have something to read and can write some letters, how bad could it be?

The answer is: very bad. Solitary confinement can cause terrible psychological harm; it causes a type of disorder that attacks the mind from the inside. Take, for instance, the work of psychologist Craig Haney.[6] For decades, he has been studying inmates who've been placed in isolation wards. Haney's accounts of what happens to such people are raw and gruesome. During a stint in solitary confinement, one man became so distraught that he stitched up his lips with a bit of thread. Another man gnawed off one of his fingers, sliced open his foot, and managed to detach his testicles. Still another man began eating his television. The guards had to pump that inmate's stomach, and after the authorities returned the inmate to his cell, he went right back to devouring his electronics.

People who come out of solitary confinement often recover. Once they engage with others again, they feel better. Their sense of self returns. This all seems to have a straightforward cause: When we have no one to bond with, when we have no one to trust, our brains can self-destruct. It's not exactly clear why this happens. But what's certain is that we have a profound urge to connect to others. We have a constant need to socialize. Or as psychologist Michael Gazzaniga once argued, "We are a bunch of party animals."[7]

This instinct to form groups has a long evolutionary history. For our distant Paleolithic cousins, other people meant safety and protection, and research suggests that primates traveling in smaller clans have less security against predators.[8] In fact, the pain of being alone seems to have evolved to shield us from the hazards of actually being alone.[9] What's more, our neural circuits evolved to be groupish. The process of navigating our social ties is baked into our brains.[10] Or as social physiologist Matthew Lieberman argues, "This is what our brains were wired for: reaching out to and interacting with others." So, for example, most of us struggle to multiply 78 times 38 in our heads, even though, as math problems go, it's not very difficult.[11] In contrast, if I were to show you a picture of your kindergarten class, I'd bet that you'd be able to recognize the faces of everyone in the class. I'd also wager that you'd be able to tell me who threw sand, who picked his nose, and who rubbed your back after you wet your pants.

To put it differently, we have a lot of the highly networked bee in our nature, and rather than viewing ourselves as the rational ape, we'd be better off thinking of ourselves, as psychologist Jonathan Haidt recommends, as "ninety percent chimp and ten percent bee."[12] Because, like bees, we can become part of something bigger, something hive-ish. Or, as Haidt writes, "We are selfish primates who long to be a part of something larger and nobler than ourselves."

To paraphrase Haidt, then, we are the gregarious ape, the supersmart lemming, and for many of us, trust is an emotive urge. Psychologist Roderick Kramer describes this as "presumptive trust," and when the investor sends money in a game like Split or Steal, the person is essentially saying: *Be part of my group.*[13] *Let's work together. Let's be friends.* And even the smallest signal of affability can build up a sense of faith, and Kramer notes that just a minor social signal like a handshake will make people more trusting. Psychologist Robert Kurzban once had players give each other a bit of eye contact in a Split or Steal–like experiment, and that alone was enough to boost the levels of cooperation.[14] Think about that for a second. Just some eye contact can create a feeling of bonding. The idea that our social ways are behind our trusting ways dates back hundreds of years. But recent research has made it clear that we have a deep need to connect to others. For humans, trust is a type of social instinct.

During World War II, the U.S. Army hoped to answer the question: Why do men fight?[15] The question should have been easy to answer —

we've been fighting wars for thousands of years. But the question of bravery is harder than it seems, and at the start of World War II, the army didn't have a reliable approach for inspiring its new recruits. Generals seemed to think that bravery was a mix of self-interest and patriotism, and when studies suggested that morale was low, the army often tried to appeal to the soldiers' inner egos. They talked about pride and changed pay structures and created a point system so that soldiers could figure out when they would be discharged. General George C. Marshall also brought in film director Frank Capra to make a movie that would explain the causes of the war. Almost every incoming soldier saw the resulting film, *Why We Fight,* which argued that World War II was about liberty and American security. Put simply, the men were supposed to be fighting the Nazis to save themselves and their way of life.

But the army also knew that might not be enough, so in the 1940s, it tapped sociologist Samuel Stouffer to study the issue of bravery. Stouffer launched a massive research project, surveying some 500,000 enlisted men, and it turned out that the men didn't fight because of patriotism or money or fear of Nazi domination. For them, the war wasn't about saving American liberty. Instead, the men fought because they believed in each other, and when Stouffer asked soldiers what kept them going, their most common response was finishing the job so that they could return to the States. But the second most common response — and the "primary combat motivation" — was a sense of connection to others.[16]

Stouffer's finding might seem odd at first glance. The men were terrified for their lives. They faced mortar rounds and sniper fire, dive-bombings and artillery attacks, Panzers and bombers. Why would their buddies make a difference? Well, trust can provide a type of well-being, a feeling of emotional support, and when you are jumping out of a foxhole, when you expect a bullet in the chest, when a German tank might kill you at any moment, faith in others can seem like the only thing that matters. A few years ago, Leonard Wong, of the United States Army War College, re-created Stouffer's study, and the findings held up. As one infantryman told Wong, "You have got to trust [other soldiers] more than your mother, your father, or girlfriend, or your wife, or anybody. It becomes almost like your guardian angel."[17]

For the most part, we don't see others as the solution to our problems — or as central to our future well-being. But our social bonds sustain us, and people with deeper social ties live longer and are less likely to die of a heart attack or cancer.[18] They're also less likely to be anxious or depressed. They're even less likely to catch a cold. Studies also suggest that people with deeper social connections are more effective at work, and individuals with warmer relationships can earn almost twice as much money as their less connected counterparts.

Why does this happen? Why would working with others give us any sort of support at all? There isn't a simple explanation. Part of the reason, it seems, is that when we're connected with others, we gain more information, which helps us solve problems more easily. By bonding with others, we also feel better about our group. And then there are our brains, and it turns out that when we connect with others, our opiates can kick in and give us a bit of joy. In a way, we know this already, as neuroscientist Patricia Churchland points out, and we have feel-good interactions with other people all the time. At work, at home, in school, we chatter with someone for a few moments and feel a little surge of happiness. Churchland admits that this isn't a real "high," but it does seem that for our brains, bonding can sometimes be its own reward.

It's easy to get carried away here, and we're not built to place our faith in everyone, as we'll see later in this book. But the bottom line is that social trust is a type of binding tissue, the so-called lubricant of society, and in the end, our social ties are what support us. I wanted to learn more about this idea and its connection to trust, and so I went to Yerkes National Primate Research Center. The field station sits a few dozen miles north of Atlanta, down a long road, nestled within a glade of pine trees. When I visited on a summer afternoon, the high-pitched screams of the primates pierced the air, as if the sounds of a far-off African jungle had been piped into the Georgia landscape. Inside the gates, some chimpanzees tussled on a football field–sized playground. Further inside, a few rhesus monkeys swung on a large climbing structure with ladders and tires and ropes.

I went to Yerkes to talk with primatologist Frans de Waal.[19] On the day that I arrived, de Waal wore a T-shirt and shorts. His white hair was cut short. Together we climbed a tall tower, which overlooked the jungle gym–like chimpanzee enclosure, and de Waal pointed out a young female chimp who was teasing an adult with a long branch.

"She's testing out her boundaries," de Waal explained. For de Waal, this wasn't a big deal. Squabbles are inevitable. More important was that after a quarrel occurs, chimps will typically comfort the victims of the fight, hugging and touching them. "We call it consolation behavior," de Waal told me. "We see it every day."

Consolation runs on empathy, according to de Waal, and researchers like de Waal define empathy as the ability to feel someone else's feelings. As an idea, empathy covers more than that, and for de Waal, the notion of empathy also includes another talent called perspective taking, or the ability to think what others are thinking. Empathy runs deep within our mammalian DNA, and many animals — mice, rats, dogs — appear to feel the feelings of others.

In humans, though, empathy seems particularly strong. In his office, de Waal showed me a video of contagious yawning among chimpanzees, and I soon found myself yawning. What's more, our empathy is a type of deep-seated social compass, and de Waal pointed out that chimps are more likely to contagiously yawn in response to someone within their group than someone outside of it.

"So I would be more likely to contagiously yawn for my wife than for a stranger?" I asked.

De Waal nodded. "This is all related to very basic levels of empathy."

But there's another lesson, just as important — it turns out that we need empathy to work in a group, according to de Waal. Without some sense of the feelings of our partners, without some sort of connection to them, it's nearly impossible to cooperate with them, and when we walk for a moment in someone else's loafers or moccasins or clogs, we can better understand what he or she wants. Or to paraphrase de Waal: We need to know the thoughts of a colleague in order to figure out if he or she needs our help. Within a small group, people need to know what their allies are thinking so that they can collaborate with them more closely.

What's more, empathy makes us more trustworthy. Or look at it like this: Trust often relies on the principle of reciprocity. I do something for you, you do something for me, and we reciprocate all the time. But self-interested reciprocity is not enough. It's too shortsighted, and if you're logical and playing something like Split or Steal, you shouldn't trust the other person. It's too likely that he'll cheat you.

Our emotions help solve this problem, as economist Robert Frank suggests.[20] We are motivated by more than the assurance that we will receive something in return — we also don't want to feel the hurt of others. In other words, empathy and its prosocial cousins — sympathy, compassion, affection — make us act in a more trustworthy way. They serve as a type of "impulse-control device," as Frank argues.

In this sense, it's empathy — along with the rest of our social emotions — that ultimately makes society possible. Philosopher Peter Singer has argued that our earliest ancestors probably felt a sense of empathy only for the people in their clan.[21] But over time, Singer argues, our circle of morality grew larger, and today we feel even for other species because once we start to empathize with others, it's hard to stop. "Were we incapable of empathy — of putting ourselves in the position of others and seeing that their suffering is like our own — then ethical reasoning would lead nowhere," Singer writes.[22] "If emotion without reason is blind, then reason without emotion is impotent."

We don't want to have empathy for everyone. No one does, and computer simulations show that trust and cooperation move in cycles.[23] Empathy might start a partnership — and everyone might become more reliable and honest — but sooner or later, someone will decide to look out for his own interests. A person will steal or cheat or just take advantage of the system. And if you're stuck in a group of untrustworthy people, it pays to distrust. When you're surrounded by selfish, unempathetic rogues, the best approach is to be a selfish, unempathetic rogue. But the cooperative instinct always seems to appear again, according to research by mathematical biologist Martin Nowak, and, in the end, our trusting ways run so deep that we even have brain circuits devoted to working with others.[24] There's a lot that scientists don't know about these circuits. But remarkably, the story of these circuits starts in many ways with a hamster-like animal known as the prairie vole.[25]

Researchers sometimes refer to prairie voles as common pests, and what's ultimately interesting about the animals is that they're deeply committed to each other. Female voles spend more than a third of their time in contact with their partners. Males will give up more than half of their day caring for their offspring. Or, as science writer Steven Johnson argues in his wonderful book *Mind Wide Open*, voles are "one of the natural world's great romantics."[26]

Some years ago, a few biologists at the University of Illinois wanted to better understand why this happened, and so they began studying the voles, keeping the rodents in cages, giving them rabbit food, and running experiments on them with various hormones. The findings were notable, especially when it came to a peptide known as oxytocin. At the time, researchers didn't know all that much about the chemical, and most experts thought that oxytocin was a simple pregnancy hormone that promoted stronger contractions during the birthing process.

Neuroscientist Sue Carter was one of the pioneers of the vole research, and she told me that she had long known that oxytocin was an important chemical. In fact, doctors had given Carter oxytocin when she was giving birth to her son. But it took study after study to show just how central the hormone was to creating a sense of connection among the voles. "We spent ten years just proving that this was a true social bond and that oxytocin played a role in it," Carter told me.

Others soon began building on Carter's work, and by the late 1990s, researchers had gone a long way to understanding the bonding mechanisms of the small animals. They knew that the oxytocin circuit was a primordial one, dating back some 100 million years. They also knew that many other chemicals and biological systems played a key role. Male voles, for instance, stopped caring for their children only if both vasopressin and oxytocin receptors were shut down, as Carter told me.

But a bigger issue remained: Were humans any different? And what would it mean if they were?

Those questions buzzed across Paul Zak's mind the first time that he heard about oxytocin. He was sitting in a shuttle bus at the time, heading to a conference south of Reno, Nevada. As the woodland of pines and junipers roared past his window, Zak began talking with the woman sitting next to him.[27] She turned out to be an anthropologist who studied the science of love, and when she heard that Zak studied trust and social capital, she asked, "Have you ever thought about studying oxytocin?"

Back then, Zak didn't know all that much about oxytocin. This was long before Zak tickled my chest to show me that the sternum has lots of oxytocin receptors. This was long before he flew to Papua New Guinea to see if oxytocin spiked before and after men performed a tribal dance. At the time, Zak's area of expertise was econometrics, not neuroscience, and he had recently shown that economic growth jumps by almost 1 percent for every 15 percent increase in trust.[28]

When Zak got back to his hotel later that day, he logged into a medical database and began reading the research on prairie voles. As he glanced through the studies, he couldn't get away from the nagging sense that the effect of oxytocin bore a significant resemblance to trust.[29] They both involve a quieting feeling, a sense of safety and comfort. In his book *The Moral Molecule,* Zak recalls thinking, "What if bonding in voles and trust in humans were actually based on the same chemistry? What if oxytocin was, in fact, the chemical signature for that elusive bonding force [Adam] Smith had called mutual sympathy?"

It took time and research and practice, but eventually Zak started running his own oxytocin experiments. One of his very first studies was straightforward: He had undergraduates play a Split or Steal–type game and afterward took samples of their blood. The results showed an unambiguous relationship between the level of faith among the players and the amount of oxytocin in their blood.[30] But that experiment alone didn't prove anything, as Zak notes. It didn't show that oxytocin actually caused the players to trust each other. It didn't mean that we were like prairie voles, who have a clear, hormonally based system for bonding with others.

Zak wanted to prove the connection conclusively. But at the time, the FDA didn't make it easy for researchers to use oxytocin inhalers. Zak didn't want to wait, though. A self-proclaimed recovering jock,

Zak is a doer. He has a warm, brawny personality, the sort of guy who even in his fifties will take off his shirt during a lecture and rub testosterone on his bare shoulders just to make a point. (It helps that Zak has the muscular build of a college basketball player.) Or consider what happened when I first reached out to Zak. I came across the neuroeconomist's research in a wonderful profile of Zak that Adam Penenberg had written for *Fast Company*, and I wanted to find out more about oxytocin's connection to trust.[31] So I emailed Zak and told him that I was working on a book on our faith in others. He wrote back and said simply: "I'm your guy."

So instead of slowly wading through the lengthy FDA-approval process, Zak began working with a group of European researchers. One of the psychologists, Markus Heinrichs, had also run some groundbreaking oxytocin experiments on humans, and together the researchers conducted the first oxytocin-infusion study on people, spritzing some fifty male investors with the chemical and giving another fifty or so a placebo before they played an economics game.[32]

The data were clear. Of the oxytocin sniffers, more than 40 percent showed the maximum amount of trust. In contrast, just 21 percent of the control group did. Plus, the average money transfer was more than 15 percent higher in the oxytocin-spritzed group. Think about it this way: If I had given you a dash of oxytocin before you played the Split or Steal game on the TV game show, you'd be more likely to trust the person that you had just met.

According to Zak, the group of researchers showed for the first time that the hormone actually caused people to place their faith in strangers, and soon overly eager science reporters wrote stories describing the "peptide of love." Television shows heralded the discovery of a trust hormone. But despite all the headlines and all the breathless articles, the real news seems to have been buried: Humans have a built-in system for trusting others.

The wet cocktail of oxytocin seemed stuck in my throat. I shook my head and sputtered for a bit, blinking my eyes, waiting for the room to come back into focus. I was at a science lab at Claremont Graduate University, thirty-five miles east of Los Angeles. One of Zak's colleagues, psychologist Jorge Barraza, stood above me, slowly counting off the seconds until he would again fill my nasal cavity with doses of the chemical.

"Okay?" he said.

I nodded.

On that afternoon, Barraza pushed less than a teaspoon of the chemical into my sinuses, and as I sat there in the lab waiting for the hormone to take hold, I wondered what the trust hormone would feel like. Would I see everyone in a gauzy halo of saintly light? Would I suddenly trust my auto mechanic to perform eye surgery? But in the end, the oxytocin didn't inspire a buzz of uninhibited trust. There were no luminous blazes. Adam Penenberg described the experience as a "fuzzy feeling." Barraza told me the effects were "maybe like having half a beer," and for me, honestly, I'm not sure that I felt anything at all.[33]

A shot of wet chemicals isn't how we usually get a boost of oxytocin, though, and while the science of the hormone is still developing, researchers believe that the chemical is released when we feel a sense of empathy.[34] When people experience an emotional connection or a sense of personal engagement, the hormone will kick into gear. Even something as simple as petting your dog can promote oxytocin release.[35] And it's in this sense that the hormone appears to play a crucial role in our urge to care for others.[36] Or as one neurobiologist, Carsten de Dreu, told me, oxytocin is "truly a social glue."[37]

By itself, though, the hormone generally produces a bit of a relaxing sensation. The amygdala is one of the most ancient parts of the brain, and it works as a type of fear-tracking device. It tells us what to worry about. Oxytocin appears to influence the area, dialing down our sense of panic and dread. At the same time, oxytocin highlights social cues, and the hormone makes people stare longer into another person's eyes.[38] With a bit of oxytocin, people are also better at figuring out if a stranger's face is angry or weepy or just frankly bored.[39]

But in the end, much of oxytocin's hormonal strength lies within a larger system of social bonding, and what's ultimately powerful about oxytocin is that it works in concert with other pleasure chemicals, such as dopamine. Oxytocin, it seems, serves as a type of systems manager, helping to oversee the hormones that make trust an enjoyable experience, according to neuroscientist Larry Young. The prairie voles provide a chemical recipe for how this works, argues Young, and it seems that there's oxytocin to orchestrate an emotional memory — and a dose of dopamine to make it feel pleasurable.

One summer afternoon, I visited Young at Emory University to find out more. Young worked in a large corner office containing the typical researcher's paraphernalia: graphing calculator, weighty statistics books. But there were also items that would look more at home in a sex therapist's office: a copy of the *Kama Sutra,* a bottle of Ménage à Trois wine. Because for Larry Young, everything goes back to sex, love, and mothering.

The important thing to remember is that evolution is a stingy process, and over time it seems to have recycled our brain circuits devoted to mother-child bonding for other purposes. Put differently, the urge that makes women care for their children became used to sweeten the social ties that keep cooperation going. Young calls this the "mommy circuit," and he believes it's the evolutionary engine behind much of our prosocial ways.

"With these other animals that have oxytocin being released in the brain, it's there to make the mother think that this baby is the most important thing in the world, and I'll do whatever I need to do to take care of that child," Young told me that afternoon, cradling his arms as if he held an imaginary child. "It all sort of originates from that need to direct the mother's attention to the baby." This helps explain why oxytocin works within the brain's broader reward system. Or, as Young told me, "You have the beginning, reward reinforcement, a feel-good kind of pleasure, and then it's maintained because 'I don't really feel good when I'm not around you.'"

A few years ago, Paul Zak flew to England to conduct an experiment. At the time, science writer Linda Geddes was getting married, and she asked Zak to find out if the ceremony would cause oxytocin to spike in herself, in her groom, and among her guests.[40] Geddes's wedding was held in a thirty-bedroom baronial mansion in one of England's rural corners, and among the damask curtains, Oriental carpets, and flutes of champagne, Zak took some blood from some of the ceremony's more scientifically inclined guests. Then, right after the wedding ended, he did it all again. It was what Geddes called "a big fat nerd wedding."

After the ceremony, Geddes wondered if her oxytocin levels had gone up at all. After all, a marriage ceremony can be deeply stressful. Zak noted something different: Weddings are a celebration of social bonding, which suggested that oxytocin might increase for everyone who attended. And when the results finally came in a month or so later, there were some wrinkles: The results turned out to line up with how people viewed the event, as Zak suggests, and the bride and groom, along with their close family members, showed clear jumps in their levels of the hormone. But friends of the bride and groom had much less of a gain — and some showed no change at all.

It was a non-experiment experiment. Only thirteen people participated in the exercise. There was no control group or peer review or testing of a hypothesis. But the anecdote underscores the conditional effects of the chemical. It's contingent on personality and context and situation.[41] After a few of the first oxytocin experiments, some believed the hormone might help people with social disorders such as autism. But oxytocin's effects appear to be too dependent on other factors for it to be an off-the-shelf cure, according to researchers like Jennifer Bartz, and while some companies are experimenting with potential applications, it will likely be years before an oxytocin-inspired medical treatment hits the market.

Part of the issue is that one's point of view can alter oxytocin's social power. Consider, for instance, this experiment: Some European researchers gave a shot of the hormone to two groups of men.[42] One group was made up of single men; the other group contained men in steady relationships. The researchers then had the two groups engage with an attractive woman. The results? The committed men stood about six inches farther away from the good-looking woman than the uncommitted men.

In other words, oxytocin is not the hormone of unending trust, as Zak himself notes, and the hormone doesn't always have a trustworthy effect. Some, like science writer Ed Yong, have criticized Zak for calling oxytocin the "moral molecule," and Yong cites experiments in which oxytocin makes people behave in immoral ways.[43] One study by Carsten de Dreu shows, for instance, that oxytocin actually made Dutch men more biased against people with Middle Eastern–sounding names.[44] For his part, Zak argues that his critics have not read his work closely enough. Oxytocin is "our social interaction and reciprocation molecule that in many, but not all, circumstances increases moral behaviors," Zak told me.

In the end, what's clear is that the recent research on oxytocin makes it easy to believe that trust is like money: Either you have it or you don't. But a closer look at the science suggests that our faith in others is like knowing how to code or cook: It's something that we learn over time, something that we need to practice, an expression of our skills and background. When Jennifer Bartz describes the effects of oxytocin, she argues that "context and person matter," and in many ways, the same can be said of trust. It is about who we are as individuals — and the contexts in which we've learned to place our faith in others.

But there's another, just as important conclusion from the oxytocin research: Our faith in others is something deeply human.[45] Or, as Zak argues, our faith in others is a part of us, something sparked by our engagement with others. It seems that this notion holds true when trust is an emotional urge. But it also turns out to be at the very center of trust's logical underpinnings. Up until now, we've been exploring the social side of our faith in others. We've looked at our groupish instincts and tried to better understand the role that our brains play in promoting our cooperative ways. But trust doesn't always start with empathy. Sometimes trust is a belief, an expectation of results, a bit of calculation-based faith, and that story begins, oddly enough, more than 150 years ago in a rocky limestone outcropping in the mountains of Tennessee.

Chapter 2

Reciprocity, Indirect Reciprocity, and What We Can Learn from Hector Ramirez

I T WAS the late afternoon of December 28, 1862, in Stewarts Creek, Tennessee. By then, the American Civil War had been raging for almost two years, and the festive, let's-go-to-war parades were long forgotten. There were no more easy recruiting days, when so many men tried to enlist in the army that the officers sent them home. Politicians on both sides had expected that the war would be over quickly. At the First Battle of Bull Run, families had come from Washington, D.C., to watch the conflict with bottles of champagne, as if it were some sort of tourist attraction. But by 1862, following one carnage-filled battle after another, the generals had no idea when the conflict would end. Another year? Another decade?

On that December day, a small group of Union soldiers stood guard near Stewarts Creek. The soldiers must have known that another battle with the Confederates would occur within days. Some two months before, the two armies had clashed in Perryville, Kentucky, where some regiments lost more than half of their men to casualties.[1] "The ground before my line of battle was literally covered with the dead and dying," recalled one officer.[2] The North had won that daylong shootout, and now in the middle of Tennessee, the armies were scheduled for a rematch.

While the Union soldiers sat in their guard post on that day, they occasionally fired at some of the gray uniforms on the other side of the creek.[3] But then, once night had fallen, one of the Union soldiers yelled over to the Confederates: "Halloo, boys. What regiment?"

"Eighth Confederate!" a man yelled back. "What's your regiment?"

"Eighth and Twenty-first Kentucky," the Union soldier replied. Then he asked, "Boys, have you got any whiskey?"

"Plenty of her."

"How'll you trade for coffee?"

"Would like to accommodate you, but never drink it."

"Let's meet at the creek and have a social chat," the Union soldier offered.

"Will you shoot?"

"Upon the honor of a gentleman, not a man shall. Will you shoot?" the Union soldier replied.

"I give you as good assurance."

"Enough said. Come on."

The men scampered down to the creek, leaving their guns behind. They must have been frightened. Would this be a trap? Would they all get killed? But there was reason to have faith in the enemy when it came to these sorts of agreements. By then, informal truces between the warring sides had become regular occurrences. Sometimes the men from the two armies would meet to play cards. On other occasions, they'd exchange trinkets for tobacco. Once, at the Battle of Fredericksburg, Union and Confederate soldiers used toy boats to make exchanges across the Rappahannock River.[4] And on that December night, the two groups of men stepped down to the creek at about the same time.

"Halloo, boys! How do you make it?" one of the Confederates yelled over. The men soon started to talk politics. They exchanged compliments and taunts in the way that only enemy soldiers can.

"Boys, are you going to make a stand at Murfreesboro?" one Union soldier asked.

"That is a leading question" came the reply. "I will venture to say it will be the bloodiest ten miles you ever traveled."

A Confederate captain joined the group and asked the Union soldiers if they had a newspaper to trade. The Union soldiers said that they didn't have any newspapers, but the captain decided to give them his paper anyway, wrapping it in a stone and tossing it across the creek. The men knew, of course, that this truce would not last, and eventually they decided to end their little armistice.

"Good-bye, boys," the men shouted as they scrambled out of the creek. "If ever I meet you in battle, I'll spare you."

The soldiers returned to their positions, and weeks later, after the Battle of Murfreesboro killed more than three thousand, one of the soldiers told a newspaper reporter from the *Nashville Dispatch* about the late-night truce: "So we met and parted, not realizing we were enemies."[5]

Why did the truce at Stewarts Creek occur? After all, war-hardened soldiers are not supposed to put down their guns for late-night gatherings. In general, people aren't eager to talk with someone who has been trying to kill them. But informal wartime truces have been going on for centuries, as military historians Malcolm Brown and Shirley Seaton have found.[6] During the Napoleonic Wars, British and French troops would sit around campfires and drink. In the Crimean War, enemy soldiers would sometimes meet for a smoke. The largest unauthorized truce happened during World War I, when a cease-fire spread across much of the five-hundred-mile Western Front on Christmas Day, and as many as 100,000 soldiers met in front of their trenches. "It is rare for a conflict at close quarters to continue very long without some generous gestures between enemies or an upsurge in the 'live and let live' spirit," write Brown and Seaton.

The engine behind many of these truces is clear: It's a matter of reciprocity. If a man does not shoot at you, you do not shoot at him. If a man gives you a smoke, you give him a smoke. And if someone walks down to the creek without a gun, you do, too. What does this have to do with trust? A lot, actually, because trust is more than a soft and fuzzy emotion. In the first chapter, I explained some of the science behind our trusting ways, arguing that our faith in others is a very human sort of bond. In this chapter, I'll look into why we trust, and I hope to show you how the principle of reciprocity — and its variations — can give an important logic to our faith in others. I also want to discuss some of the other ways that societies make people act in the group's best interest, as well as examine some others security expert Bruce Schneier identifies as "societal pressures."

For right now, though, let's go back to Split or Steal, which is basically a stripped-down version of the famed Prisoner's Dilemma. Over the years, the dilemma has been the subject of a dozen books, hundreds of articles, and countless research studies. It has also been the name of a rock band and the focus of an art exhibit, and it even inspired a short film. The dilemma provides a way to think about a complex set of questions: When should we work with others?[7] When should we look out for ourselves? And if it pays to be a jerk — at least in the short term — why should someone ever be nice?

Political scientist Robert Axelrod remembers the first moment he came across the dilemma. He was in college. It was the 1960s. He was reading a book called *Games and Decisions,* and the essential idea posed by the dilemma fascinated him. Then, over a decade later, Axelrod developed a hunch that reciprocity might reveal a solution, and with the help of some game theorists, Axelrod showed that the strategy known as tit for tat — which is essentially the principle of reciprocity — was the most effective approach.

Axelrod himself is not a revolutionary guy. He sports ocean-blue sweater-vests and wears his hair in a soft comb-over. In high school, he was fascinated by computer-based checkers. But Axelrod's discovery was dramatic. "The most fascinating point was that tit for tat won the tournaments even though it could never do better than the player it was interacting with," Axelrod once wrote.[8] "Instead it won by its success at eliciting cooperation."

One part of tit for tat's success is that the approach is trustworthy. So if you show a bit of trust, the strategy of reciprocity will return that favor. And then there's the structure of the game itself. The dilemma is what economists call a non-zero-sum game.[9] In a zero-sum game, only one side can be victorious. It's a matter of win or lose, pass or fail. But the dilemma is different, especially when it's played repeatedly, and it contains win-win situations as well as win-lose situations. And in this way, the game models real-life interactions. When you buy shoes, when you take a Spanish class, when you play Split or Steal on a game show, these are all non-zero-sum interactions. Within this framework, everyone can win, as Axelrod notes. Everyone can lose, too, and what tit for tat did was provide a way for both sides to win.

Reciprocity, then, is more than a way for soldiers to create informal truces. With a bit of kindness, it can become a strategy of cooperation — and build trust where trust might never otherwise occur.

When Pierre Omidyar started eBay on a Sunday afternoon in the summer of 1995, almost no one thought that the website would eventually become one of the largest companies in the world. At the time, the notion of buying things online from a stranger seemed bizarre, as Adam Cohen recounts in his book *The Perfect Store*.[10] Back then, people went online to send emails and check discussion boards like Usenet. Only a few people trusted websites enough to provide them with a credit card number.[11]

Omidyar didn't have grand hopes for the site either. In his mind, he thought of eBay as a way of testing out an idea. "People were doing business with one another through the Internet already, through bulletin boards," he explained.[12] "But on the Web, we could make it interactive, we could create an auction, we could create a real marketplace. And that's really what triggered my imagination."

In the early days, eBay had the look and feel of a church newsletter. There were just a few categories — antiques, automotive, electronics — and the site seemed narrow and crowded.[13] Omidyar hosted the auction site on the back end of his personal website, and with a few clicks, users could find themselves reading about the Ebola virus, one of Omidyar's other interests.

It all changed with a broken laser pointer, according to Cohen. Omidyar had purchased the pointer sometime earlier, and he had never used it much beyond teasing his cat. After the item gave out, Omidyar listed the pointer on the site, explaining that he had purchased it for thirty dollars, and he kicked off the auction at one dollar. A few weeks — and multiple bids — later, the pointer sold for fourteen dollars, even though it was nothing more than a broken office item.

And as Omidyar wrapped the pointer to ship to the buyer, he thought that the site might just be successful, writes Cohen.

Omidyar was right, and within months, eBay had thousands of users. But as the site grew, so did the disputes. Buyers complained: Their purchases arrived broken or didn't arrive at all. Sellers got angry: Someone didn't pay up or paid late. Every day a dozen or so emails would land in Omidyar's inbox, according to Cohen, and for the most part, the arguments were over little things. "On the Internet, people forget that when they're dealing with an email address there's an actual human being on the other side," Omidyar told Cohen.[14] "Often their fears are manifested, or they jump to conclusions and think the most negative interpretations of that email."

Early on, Omidyar would email both buyer and seller and say something along the lines of *You figure it out.*[15] But as eBay grew, Omidyar understood he needed to do more, and eventually he decided to focus on an individual's reputation. Omidyar called the program the "Feedback Forum," and after a sale, users could evaluate each other with a score of plus one, minus one, or neutral. When Omidyar introduced the changes, he said in an online dispatch: "Some people are dishonest. Or deceptive. This is true here, in the newsgroups, in the classifieds, and right next door. It's a fact of life. But here, those people can't hide. We'll drive them away."[16]

When Omidyar launched the Feedback Forum, it wasn't at all clear that the approach would succeed. After all, it often takes time — and guts — to write a negative review. Omidyar also worried that it "might just turn into a gripe forum."[17] But reviews soon began to flood the site, and Omidyar's feedback system became one of the central drivers of eBay's success.[18] Today, of course, the idea of a rating system seems obvious, and online reviews are central to all sorts of websites. But Omidyar's system was groundbreaking, and for a long time, many observers were doubtful that the feedback system would even work.

This matters because there's another piece of logic behind our trusting ways. So far, we've seen how reciprocity can explain cooperation between two strangers. But it turns out that reciprocity has a corollary that might be more powerful than tit for tat, and it's called indirect reciprocity. So if reciprocity is a matter of "I scratch your back, you scratch mine," indirect reciprocity is a matter of "If I scratch your back, someone else will scratch mine."[19] With indirect reciprocity, we don't need to follow each tit for tat. Instead we work together more broadly, believing that what goes around comes around.

As an idea, indirect reciprocity has a long history. In his work, legal scholar Yochai Benkler traces the idea all the way back to Benjamin Franklin, and others, like writer Howard Rheingold, have pointed out the connection between the rise of eBay and trust in strangers. But still, many of us are much like the observers who were doubtful of Omidyar's Feedback Forum. We underestimate how crucial the notion is to our sense of society.

To learn more about indirect reciprocity, I reached out to Martin Nowak, a mathematical biologist at Harvard, who has been studying the idea for decades. Nowak likes to joke that he sounds like Arnold Schwarzenegger. He was born in Austria; his voice is deeply sonorous. And during our conversation, Nowak argued that what's important about indirect reciprocity is that it sustains a sense of cooperation in large groups. It encourages us to "help those who help others," he told me, and so we will seek out people who are trustworthy — and stay away from people who aren't dependable.

Experts typically talk about indirect reciprocity within the framework of evolution, and it turns out that indirect reciprocity helps explain how complexity arises within the dog-eat-dog world of natural selection. Nowak goes even further, arguing that indirect reciprocity powers any large community. According to Nowak, indirect reciprocity supports specialization — and thus economic exchange — by allowing people to have faith that other people will pay it forward. "Thanks to the power of reputation, we think nothing of paying one stranger for a gift and then waiting to receive delivery from another stranger, thanks also to the efforts of various other people whom we have never met and will never meet," Nowak writes in his book *SuperCooperators*.[20] "We all depend on third parties to ensure that those who scratch backs will have theirs scratched eventually."

The lesson here is that indirect reciprocity drives trustworthiness, and the Golden Rule turns out to rest on a belief in the power of indirect reciprocity, as Nowak suggests. The Golden Rule is the idea that we should treat others like we want to be treated, and the notion often feels simpleminded, like one of those things that your kindergarten teacher told you that now feels tired and brainless — the ethical version of not running with scissors. Even so, it turns out that almost every major religion emphasizes the rule in some way.[21]

This wasn't a matter of chance. When we engage in indirect reciprocity, we're building a culture of trust. We're investing in our social capital. We're fostering a sense of society, as Robert Putnam suggests, and the Golden Rule is a way to judge trustworthy behavior. It's a moral benchmark that has been baked into our culture, and Pierre Omidyar's genius was to figure out a reliable way to transfer the force of the idea to the Internet.[22]

At the time that Omidyar founded eBay, online interactions were a lot like a society that had only direct reciprocity: Individuals trusted only the people that they knew. What Omidyar did was give users an easy way to communicate about the trustworthiness of others, giving a far larger group of people the chance to reliably place their faith in a stranger. As Omidyar once explained, the feedback system "was really the thing that allowed eBay to succeed, because it gave people a chance, a way to know that they could actually trust a complete stranger."[23]

In their book *The Art of Strategy*, Avinash Dixit and Barry Nalebuff present Charlie Brown as a way to understand game theory. You probably can recall the long-standing gag from the comic strip *Peanuts*.[24] One of the characters, Lucy van Pelt, would volunteer to hold a football for Charlie Brown as he ran to kick it. At first, Charlie would decline Lucy's offer — he knew that she was devious. But Lucy would cajole Charlie. She'd talk about the Bible and their friendship and mock his cynicism. And so Charlie would try to kick the football, and without fail, Lucy would yank the ball at the last second, and Charlie would fall on his back with an *"Aaugh!"*

In a way, Charlie Brown's problem was straightforward: He didn't know if Lucy could keep her promise. Economists sometimes refer to this idea as a "commitment problem," and in many ways there's a commitment problem in every trusting relationship, since you never know for sure if the other person will deliver on his promise.[25] Money, reputation, jail time — they all can help solve commitment problems. But it also turns out that culture is a way to ensure commitment.[26]

Let's start, though, with the Great New York City Parking War. The conflict began in New York City in the 1990s, when representatives from the United Nations would declare diplomatic immunity in order to get out of paying for parking tickets.[27] Over time, the foreign attachés racked up more than 150,000 tickets, and many of the violations were egregious. The diplomats parked in loading zones. They left their cars in front of fire hydrants. The fines totaled more than eighteen million dollars, and eventually Mayor Michael R. Bloomberg and Secretary of State Colin L. Powell hammered out a truce.[28]

The parking war faded from the headlines until two economists, Ray Fisman and Edward Miguel, began studying the data to figure out who exactly incurred all the unpaid tickets.[29] The academics wanted to know who followed the law when there were no rules — when individuals had total immunity — and who did not. The outcome was conclusive: The diplomats from relatively corruption-free Scandinavian countries had the least number of unpaid tickets.

The offenders? They were the diplomats from the more corrupt nations, and the attachés from Chad and Bangladesh each had more than a thousand violations. In other words, the diplomats seemed to have brought a bit of home with them to New York City, and if their own country had high levels of corruption, they were far more likely to park illegally. "A certain amount of corruption is grounded in culture," Fisman concluded.[30]

To paraphrase Fisman, a certain amount of our trust — and trustworthiness — is grounded in culture, and while it's easy to dismiss culture as a matter of traditions and customs, it turns out that our social fabric can become a central part of our mental process. When we grow up in a society in which cooperation is the norm, the decision to trust — and be trustworthy — can become automatic.

A few years ago, Harvard University psychologist David Rand conducted a powerful study looking at why people cooperate, and he brought in as many subjects as he could to play the Prisoner's Dilemma.[31] Some of the subjects were Boston-area undergraduates. Others were young people from around the globe who played the game online. Rand ultimately enrolled almost two thousand people in the experiment, and he administered the game under a variety of conditions. Some people played the game impulsively; others he pushed to think deliberately. When I met Rand at his office, he had just landed a professorship at Yale University, and he told me that his lab's motto would be "We didn't come here to fuck around."

So what were the results of this psychologist with the brash lab motto? It turns out that our intuitive ways may be some of our best commitment devices. Our raw, emotional impulse is to reciprocate, and when Rand primed people to think about their intuitions, they were far more cooperative than when they were being deliberate. Speed also made a difference, and the faster that people made a decision, the more likely it was that they would be cooperative.

In Rand's study, for instance, people who took less than a half second to make a choice decided to work with their partner around 70 percent of the time. But people who took two seconds or longer supported their partner only around 40 percent. What's more, people were more cooperative if they saw more cooperation in their everyday lives. If people were told to be slow and logical, everyone was relatively selfish, according to Rand. In other words, if you tell people to think rationally, they think about themselves. But when people relied on their impulses, on their emotions, their day-to-day experiences mattered a lot, and if people said that most people were trustworthy, they were far more reflexively trusting.

What's important to keep in mind is how our brains work, and as psychologist Daniel Kahneman has shown, it's useful to think of our brains as having two cognitive systems.[32] The first system is quick and almost effortless. Call it the impulsive brain. The second system concerns itself with things that require concentration, like mathematical calculations. Call it the deliberate brain. And for the most part, the deliberate brain hangs out in the background. It's a lazy sort of beast, and the impulsive brain generally pushes the deliberate brain into action only when it comes across a problem that it doesn't know how to solve.

What Rand's study suggests is that our sense of trust can become embedded within our impulsive brains. It can become a type of emotional, knee-jerk reaction. I started this chapter by explaining some of the intellectual framework behind our social instincts, that reciprocity can work to build a sense of faith in others even in a world that's filled with selfish individuals, and there's no question that the idea remains accurate.

But it seems that our social fabric can help trust become a sort of instinct. According to popular wisdom, we work with others because we decide it's the right thing to do. We engage in a type of calculation-based trust, deliberately weighing the gains of defection and cooperation. But it doesn't always work that way; just recall the Civil War truce. The soldiers who were on guard duty didn't seem to dwell on all of the potential consequences of their actions. They didn't appear to think much about what would happen if a Union soldier pulled out a musket or if the Confederates brought down a top general. When they yelled out for a chance to "talk it out," their opponents responded, and so they went down to the creek.

Not long ago, security expert Bruce Schneier wrote an excellent book called *Liars and Outliers* that smartly maps out the ways that people can be pressured to act in the group's self-interest.[33] In the work, Schneier argues that there are a number of crucial pressures that can "induce" trust. Schneier's work shares important connections with some of the ideas that we've already seen in this chapter. For instance, Schneier points out that morals — a psychological cousin of culture — can sustain cooperation. Schneier also argues that reputation, which is what operated within eBay, can help create compliance.

But when a system of cooperation evolves into a society, Schneier argues that we need institutions, and when we're dealing with a stranger, we're generally more trusting if we know that there is someone else who will go after a stranger who betrays us. In other words, we show more faith in others when there is a system that will mitigate the risk of placing our faith in someone else. "Institutions, formalism, rules, governance, whatever you want to call it," Schneier told me. "They exist because the group has to scale."

What's important about institutions is that they serve as a straightforward way to solve a commitment problem. By lessening the risk associated with placing our faith in someone else, they improve calculation-based forms of trust. Take something like driving on a highway. At first glance, it doesn't seem to make much sense to trust any of the other drivers. After all, they could be texting. They might not even have driver's licenses. And really, why would those drivers care about you? Or, the next time that you're on the highway, take a look around. Study the people in the car next to you. Do you know them? Do they know you? Why are you trusting them with your life? And at least for Schneier, the answer to this question is government. We trust other drivers because there are cops who arrest people who drive too fast as well as other institutional systems that ensure that people have some driving ability before they go out on the road.

This is important because if everyone drives safely, we all benefit. Some years ago, heiress Paris Hilton drank some tequila at a charity event and then roared off in her Mercedes McLaren.[34] The cops pulled Hilton over as she drove down a Hollywood street, and they knew almost immediately that she had been drinking. At her hearing some weeks later, Hilton showed a deep sense of remorse, telling the judge that "no one is above the law. I surely am not." And while Hilton's phrase is an overtaxed cliché, it underscores the point: Government helps us understand that we're all better off if we do the right thing.

But there are problems when it comes to institutional sanctions, as Schneier and others have argued, and at the heart of any large-scale effort to induce people to cooperate is a paradox. Societies create sanctions to help solve commitment problems, and people do all sorts of collective things, like not drink and drive, because they're afraid of getting caught. But at the same time, government can destroy trust. Sanctions can erode a culture of trustworthiness.

The issue is that a feeling of empowerment is central to building our faith in others. We want to work with others, but only if we choose to work with others. We want to cooperate, but only if we are not forced to cooperate. We see this in our own lives, and we're generally more motivated if we have some sense of control. This explains why people run their own companies. This explains why people choose their own hobbies. We feel more driven if we have some autonomy. Consider a recent study that found that people who lived in countries with greater economic and cultural freedoms were more trusting of strangers.

Trust, in a phrase, can't be forced. At its core, it is a deeply social act. Albert Einstein had it right when he wrote that "every kind of peaceful cooperation among men is primarily based on mutual trust and only secondly on institutions such as courts of justice and police." Paris Hilton had it right, too, when she once told *Esquire* that "trust is just a feeling that you have."[35] The problem is that sometimes we forget about this sort of faith in others. We need to be reminded. And that's why a high-flying heiress needs to go to jail for having had too much to drink before getting behind the wheel of her Mercedes. Or as Hilton told the judge: "I am ready to face the consequences" of what I did.

When it comes to "institutional pressures," there's another paradox, as Schneier suggests, and it turns out that we also don't always want people to obey the law. Sometimes there are very good reasons to run a stop sign. Sometimes it makes sense to drive through a red light, like if your partner is about to give birth. But the bigger point here is that we want people to decide moral issues for themselves, to have their own sense of right and wrong, to follow their own ethical compass, as Schneier argues.

Take the experience of Hector Ramirez. I first came across Ramirez's story in a review of Schneier's book by Jordan Ellenberg in the *Wall Street Journal*.[36] In his article, Ellenberg described Ramirez as an example of a modern-day hero, someone who broke the law in order to do the right thing. The account of what Ramirez did stayed with me. Too often, it seems, we think of heroes as people who lived in ancient Greece, a piece of antiquity that we pull out, dust off, and tell to our children.

I reached out to Ramirez, and he recounted the basics of what happened. On September 11, 2001, he was driving a subway train through lower Manhattan. Ramirez's father had worked for the New York City Transit Authority, and Ramirez himself had long dreamed of getting a job driving subway trains. After high school, Ramirez had a position cleaning trains, and eventually he worked his way up to become a train operator.

As Ramirez drove the train that morning, he received a call over the radio from the command center: He should not stop at the Cortlandt Street station. At that point, Ramirez didn't know about the planes or the towers or the terrorist attacks, so he continued on to the Cortlandt Street stop, located beneath the World Trade Center. On that morning, Ramirez planned to go through the station, honking the train's horn to alert people to step back from the platform. Typically, upon hearing the horn, riders would step back from the track's edge as Ramirez drove the train through. Sometimes people would tap their watches or give him the finger. "You know, it's New York," Ramirez told me.

But on that day, everyone on the platform looked terrified. Inside the tunnel, smoke hung in the air, bringing visibility down by about half. Still, through the gray haze, Ramirez locked eyes with one woman, her face blazing with terror. "I just saw fear," Ramirez told me. "I had never seen anything like that in my life." And so, despite what he had been told by the command center, Ramirez pulled the train to a stop. The conductor opened the doors, and people rushed into the cars. Nobody got off. As Ramirez drove out of the station, he figured he'd probably get a reprimand from his boss, if not much worse. *I've got to figure out how to write this incident report,* he thought, *because this is going to be ugly.*

When I spoke to Ramirez, he was out on sick leave for a broken shoulder. "I'd like to tell you that I laid down a motorcycle trying to avoid a deer or something like that," he said. But he broke his shoulder after a "trip and fall." And during our conversation, Ramirez recalled what happened on September 11 with an exacting memory. His story doesn't seem to have changed at all over the years, and when Ramirez tells the anecdote about driving the train through the station, it seems that he almost always includes the detail of staring into the woman's eyes.

This detail matters because it's what inspired Ramirez to do the right thing. He connected with the woman on the platform. He felt a sense of empathy, and there's no question today that Ramirez is, in fact, a hero. If Ramirez had obeyed his supervisors, if he had obeyed the law, it seems almost certain that the people standing on the platform would have died when the towers collapsed.

When I spoke to Ramirez, he explained that after he found out about the terrorist attacks, he thought of leaving work early to find out if his wife was okay. But Ramirez stayed on the job, helping people get home. It turned out that his wife had been helped by other city employees, and she eventually arrived home safely. What happened, more broadly, then, was a matter of indirect reciprocity. Ramirez did what he had to do on that day, and he told me that "my coworkers were all doing what they had to do." It was the Golden Rule at work. It was the strength of our social ties. Some like Schneier argue that societies are too large to rely only on relational types of trust. That's accurate, of course, but it overlooks just how important it is to foster the instinct to trust, to promote a culture of connectedness. In short, we need for people to act more like Hector Ramirez.

Chapter 3

How We Trust

The Lessons of Clark Rockefeller

A CCORDING TO Mark Seal's fascinating book *The Man in the Rockefeller Suit,* the SUV seemed to come out of nowhere. It was Sunday, July 27, 2008, Boston, Massachusetts. Clark Rockefeller, his daughter, and a social worker strolled down a Boston side street. Rockefeller wore deck shoes and thick Clark Kent glasses and a Yale baseball cap, according to Seal.[1] Rockefeller told people that he worked for developing countries, helping them stabilize their debts, and he appeared to have a high-powered Rolodex, brimming with high-powered friends, among them German chancellor Helmut Kohl, pop singer Britney Spears, and radio host Garrison Keillor.[2]

As Seal tells the story, Rockefeller and his wife had recently split up. According to the custody arrangement, Rockefeller could visit with his daughter only three days each year, and a social worker had to be with them at all times. On that July morning, the group ambled around the city. The weather was warm. The sky was cloudless, and for a while, the group visited a nearby park. They walked over to the Red Sox's stadium, where Rockefeller explained that he had landed excellent seats for them to watch the game that night against the Yankees.[3]

According to Seal, the three began heading down Marlborough Street, where Rockefeller directed everyone to look at some nearby construction. As social worker Howard Yaffe gazed into the distance, past the townhouses, past the facades, looking for the construction site, Rockefeller gave the man a strong push. Yaffe sprawled to the sidewalk, and Rockefeller seized his daughter and darted into the waiting vehicle. Yaffe ran after the car, but the SUV soon vanished into the Boston traffic, along with one of the biggest con men in American history.

According to Seal, the first few days of the investigation of Clark Rockefeller was like sifting through the résumé of a Hollywood actor. Over the years, Rockefeller had played the part of a half dozen people in a half dozen locations. In some places, Rockefeller ran small frauds that would have barely made the local police blotter; he once got a Las Vegas cardiologist to give him a thousand dollars to start up a medical practice, according to Seal.[4] But Rockefeller could also be cruel and vicious. In California, the con man murdered John Sohus and buried the remains in the backyard of Sohus's childhood home.

Eventually, investigators figured out that Rockefeller was really Christian Karl Gerhartsreiter. According to Seal's account, Rockefeller slipped into the United States during the Carter administration as a thick-accented Bavarian adolescent, and by the time Rockefeller kidnapped his daughter more than three decades later, he had sweet-talked his way into the world of the very rich and very famous. Rockefeller often dined with one of the elder statesmen of Boston architecture, Patrick Hickox. He became friends with John Winthrop Sears, a onetime Republican candidate for governor of Massachusetts.[5] Rockefeller owned a home in New Hampshire that had once belonged to the legal philosopher Learned Hand, and Rockefeller's wife, Sandra Boss, earned somewhere around two million dollars a year working for the McKinsey Group, one of the world's most respected consulting companies.[6]

What's important about the Rockefeller case, though, is that it helps us understand how we decide to place our faith in others, as writer Drake Bennett argued in the *Boston Globe* article that inspired this chapter, and more than anything, a swindler needs the faith of others. The point of this chapter, then, isn't to show why trust goes wrong. We'll look more at that idea in the next chapter. The point is to better understand how we earn the faith of others and how that faith plays out within our communities.

The first lesson of the case is clear: Rockefeller earned people's trust by becoming part of their group. In fact, the very first step of Rockefeller's con seems to have been to try to burrow himself into a web of social connections, and according to Seal's account, whenever the con man arrived in a new city or town, he would slowly insert himself into the local church community. In New York City, he attended the famed Saint Thomas Church just around the corner from Rockefeller Center.[7] In New Hampshire, he joined the blue-blooded Trinity Church.[8] "I met him at the Church of Our Savior, and he would be out on the patio after church, talking, looking very dapper, being very friendly," one woman told Seal.[9]

As Seal notes, Rockefeller would usually progress from churches to private clubs. He had membership cards for the India House and the Lotus Club in Manhattan.[10] In Boston he was on the board of directors of the Algonquin Club.[11] And while it might seem like Rockefeller went overboard, these sorts of connections turned out to be crucial. They gave Rockefeller access to insider knowledge, for one. Rockefeller knew which names to drop, what clothes to wear, which parties to attend. This matters more than you might think. When I once walked through Boston's esteemed Somerset Club wearing shorts and sneakers, it seemed like I had violated a major cultural rule. It felt like everyone was looking at me, as if I wore a giant "trespasser" sign on my forehead. More broadly, the point is that groups have common beliefs, shared attitudes, and those views are central to how a group understands itself. Indeed, this is part of the definition of a group, and when we think about whom to trust, we place a lot of weight on whether or not the person is within our social sphere, if they share our norms and views and perspectives, or if they have the insider knowledge that defines them as a member of our tribe.

At the same time, Rockefeller's social ties gave validity to his scam, because if a friend introduces you to someone new, you're generally going to assume that person is trustworthy.[12] Just recall the last time that you became friends with someone — you almost certainly met that person through someone else whom you trusted. We don't think of our social ties in this way, but they give us a sense of legitimacy. They give us authority.

This is also why, I'd argue, Rockefeller chose the name Rockefeller. The name must have hung over every conversation that he had, as Seal points out. It made it seem as if people should feel lucky to meet him. As the founder of Standard Oil, John D. Rockefeller was the nation's first megamillionaire, and the family remains powerful. The current patriarch, David Rockefeller, is worth $2.7 billion.[13] David's cousin Jay Rockefeller is an influential senator from West Virginia. The family even has its own venture capital firm, Venrock. Clark Rockefeller made it clear that he had access to the family's vast resources, according to Seal. In conversations, Clark Rockefeller would mention that he spent every Thanksgiving at Kykuit, the family's massive estate in New York.[14] He would tell stories about "Uncle David" and "Uncle Jay."[15] Rockefeller once told a friend that his grandparents had given him one of the family's famed yachts, *True Love*.[16] The importance of Rockefeller's surname went far beyond the money, however. For most people, in fact, the name must have signaled something far more important than cash. It showed that Rockefeller was highly networked. Rockefeller was someone who knew people who knew people, and so people placed their faith in him.

One of the most important explanations of social capital comes from Robert Putnam. In his seminal book *Bowling Alone,* Putnam argues that social capital is the amount of connectedness within a group of individuals. For Putnam, social capital is more than just the number of friends you might have on Facebook or the number of email addresses in your Gmail account; the sociologist argues that social capital is a type of groupish goodwill. In his work, Putnam also draws a distinction between types of social capital. Bonding capital, according to Putnam, is what brings groups closer together. Bridging capital is what connects us across social lines, and it seems that it was a type of bridging capital that allowed Rockefeller to push his scam. Rockefeller would use one individual to take advantage of another. Think, then, of Rockefeller's con as the con of a network.

To be sure, it doesn't seem that Rockefeller ever discussed the notion of social capital. Nor has he ever explained how he got people to trust him so much. (Rockefeller didn't respond to my efforts to interview him.) Once, however, when investigators finally caught up with him in

2008, the con man let his guard down for a few moments, according to Seal. While sitting in a small interview room, he told federal agents that the name Rockefeller held significant power.[17] "It was easy to get into the clubs, by just saying you are a Rockefeller," he told them. "It would enhance a club if a Rockefeller was on the board." His surname, Rockefeller said, had the influence of "a charm."

In the spring of 1993, Clark Rockefeller hosted a small party themed around the murder mystery board game Clue.[18] Rockefeller wanted people to arrive at the party acting out their assigned characters, according to Seal, and Rockefeller himself assumed the part of the hare-brained academic Professor Plum. He wore a set of purplish trousers and walked around holding a tumbler of sherry. Rockefeller had invited his friend Julia Boss, who brought along her sister, Sandra.

As Seal tells the story, Sandra Boss was in New York City for job interviews, and she arrived at the party as the alluring Miss Scarlet. At first glance, Sandra thought the con man was handsome, and Rockefeller seemed to almost fawn over her. Later, Sandra explained that Rockefeller "was very enthusiastic about the idea of getting to know me and being romantically involved."[19] She added, "He was very physically attentive and, you know, guys may or may not make an effort to make sure you're having a good time. He was very attentive."[20]

This doesn't seem to have been an accident. When we decide to trust someone, we rely on all sorts of information. Some of it comes from our networks. Did we get introduced to this person by a friend? Other clues come from what people say: Do we relate to what they're telling us? And then there's how people communicate: Does the person gaze into your eyes? Does the person move his head up and down as if he's agreeing with you and attentive to what you're saying?

In his *Boston Globe* story, Bennett argues that Rockefeller must have relied on a variety of subtle social cues to gain the trust of other people. Bennett notes, for instance, how certain mental shortcuts can make a difference in whom we decide to trust, and one study showed that a face with "high inner eyebrows" can make someone seem more trustworthy. Bennett also discusses the power of mimicking others, noting new research about a device called a sociometer. The sociometer looks a bit like a pack of cigarettes, and it hangs around your neck while recording all sorts of nonverbal signals, including speech patterns and body language. If you lean closer to someone to show attention, the device measures it. If you raise your voice to signal a bit of concern, the device measures it — and according to Bennett, research from the sociometer data suggests "how we say something can matter more than what we actually say."

I was intrigued by Bennett's angle on the Rockefeller case, so I began reading the work of Alex Pentland, who invented the sociometer. In his book *Honest Signals,* Pentland argues that these sorts of "social signals" constitute a "second channel" of human communication.[21] More than that, Pentland argues, the signals serve as a way to tap into our social fabric. Our social signals are processed within our unconscious brains, according to Pentland, and the cues can build the type of connection between two people that fosters a sense of trust.

Part of the power of social signals is that they underscore what we want to say. They serve as a sort of bass line to the melody of our words. If you've ever read a transcript of a conversation between two people, the importance of social signals is easy to understand. Take this snippet of a conversation from the so-called smoking gun conversation between President Richard Nixon and his chief of staff, Bob Haldeman:[22]

> President: Who the hell is Ken Dahlberg?
>
> Haldeman: He's ah, he gave $25,000 in Minnesota and ah, the check went directly in to this, to this guy Barker.
>
> President: Maybe he's a . . . bum. He didn't get this from the committee though, from Stans.
>
> Haldeman: Yeah. It is. It is. It's directly traceable and there's some more through some Texas people in — that went to the Mexican bank which they can also trace to the Mexican bank . . . they'll get their names today. And . . .
>
> President: Well, I mean, ah, there's no way . . . I'm just thinking if they don't cooperate, what do they say? They, they, they were approached by the Cubans. That's what Dahlberg has to say, the Texans, too. Is that the idea?

Haldeman: Well, if they will. But then we're relying on more and
more people all the time. That's the problem. And ah, they'll
stop if we could, if we take this other step.

President: All right. Fine.

Haldeman: And, and they seem to feel the thing to do is get them
to stop?

President: Right, fine.

Without seeing the body language of the two men, it's difficult to
figure out what is going on. Each phrase seems loose and unfinished,
and you'd probably understand about as much of what was happening
if you watched a video of their conversation without any sound. Or
recall a time when you watched a foreign film without subtitles.[23] It's
remarkable how much of the essential plot you can understand.

This is the power of social signals, and it turns out that they provide
insight into how a person is feeling or thinking. When we lean toward
the speaker, for instance, we indicate that we care. People might respond with a lack of interest and lean back, or they might show domi-
nance and cut off the other person, like Nixon does with Haldeman.

Bennett's article ran a few weeks after the Rockefeller case first made
the headlines, and I was curious. Was Bennett right? Is this really what
Clark Rockefeller did to his marks? Did the con man have a keen sense
of social signals? And it does seem that a lot of observers were struck by
how Rockefeller said things. According to one of the people he conned,
Rockefeller spoke like the millionaire Thurston Howell III from *Gil-
ligan's Island*.[24] When the *Boston Globe* sent reporters to interview
Rockefeller in jail, he bowed to each visitor, as if they were royalty.[25]

Or take the story of his acquaintance with Amy Patt.[26] She was
standing at a bus stop when Rockefeller came striding up to her, according to Seal. "Don't you look pretty today!" Rockefeller told her.
The two soon developed a friendship, hanging out at the local Starbucks together. "He would say silly things like, 'Oh, Amy, Amy, Amy,
we should have children together,'" she once explained. "'You're so
smart, and our children would be so brilliant!'" Their relationship
never became romantic, writes Seal. But Patt always thought highly of

Rockefeller, always enjoyed his company. "He was really energetic and flirty," she explained, "and just sort of fun to be around."

I wanted to learn more about social signals, so I went to Boston to meet with Ben Waber, who is the CEO of a firm that offers consulting services based on the data that comes from the sociometer. Waber studied with Pentland at MIT, and he has a bit of the look of an indie rocker — shaved head, big leather watch, checkered shirt. Waber and I sat in the company's meeting room, both wearing sociometers as we talked, as the analysis of our discussion appeared on a small screen in front of us. The results looked like a video game, with each person represented by a circle. When Waber spoke to me, a line shot from his circle to my circle, and the more he talked, the larger his circle grew.

Waber leaned back and continued to speak — his circle shooting even more lines at my circle — as he explained that social signals help bind us into small networks of friends and colleagues. These groups are intimate, and when we're angry or disappointed, we turn to the people that we know well. When Waber gave sociometers to some eighty people working in a Bank of America call center a few years ago, for instance, he found that the employees who had a close-knit group of friends were more effective — and less stressed.[27] With deeper social connections, these employees could better handle calls from irate customers, and, according to Waber, a 10 percent increase in group cohesion was the equivalent of an employee having an additional thirty years' worth of experience.

Waber let me see the power of social signals for myself, and he let me borrow a set of sociometers for a weekend so that my wife and I could test them out. At first I was worried that the devices were going to reveal something I didn't want revealed, and I felt like I was going to visit a marriage counselor who would have hard numbers on my various shortcomings. Would I be shown to be a pain-in-the-ass nudge? Would I be the sort of guy who always interrupts his wife? But despite a couple of fraught events — such as my seven-year-old daughter's birthday party — the data was positive. My wife and I didn't seem to interrupt each other all that much, and at least on one of the days, it seemed that my wife and I spent a good amount of time mimicking each other. As Waber told me, during those times, "it would imply that you were really in sync."

But what's interesting about social signals is that they do more than bind us to our partners. They also link us into a much larger circle of people; they give us a way to relate to people who might be outside of our network. Or think of them as a way to create a type of bridging capital. In one project, Waber and his team used sociometers to track people in a company as they ate lunch.[28] Some people went to a café that had small tables. Others went to a cafeteria that had large, twelve-person tables. It turned out that the people who sat at the big tables were more effective employees. They were also better able to handle difficult events such as downsizing. "When you eat lunch with somebody, not surprisingly, you're much more likely to talk to that person later in the day and later in the week," Waber told me. So, for instance, if Bob in sales has an administrative issue, he's far better off if he's had lunch a few times with Jeff in human resources. It gives Bob access to more information and faster, more innovative ways of getting things done.

There's little question that social ties helped Rockefeller promote his scam. Just consider the fact that Rockefeller didn't have a Social Security card or a driver's license, according to Seal. Rockefeller also often had acquaintances pay for him and drive for him.[29] His large group of connections was particularly helpful when he went on the run, and before he kidnapped his daughter, Rockefeller had told some people that he was going to Alaska for a while.[30] Others believed that he was heading to South Africa. Still others thought that he was going sailing.[31] It made the first few days of the investigation a mess of false leads and bad tips.

As part of my reporting, I reached out to one of Rockefeller's friends, architect Patrick Hickox. In his book, Seal describes a fascinating interview with Hickox. The two men talked over wine and oysters, and in his remarks to Seal, Hickox argued that Rockefeller was a "genuine fraud." I was intrigued by Hickox's comment, and so I met up with the architect at a Mexican place just off Harvard Square.

Hickox arrived a minute or two late, bursting through the front door of the restaurant with the flair of an aging matinee idol. He wore a Burberry overcoat and a thin, silken scarf. His white hair fell around his face in a thick pageboy.

You look exactly like yourself, Hickox said as he stretched out his hand.

I hope so, I replied.

Well, given the conversation, this is important, he said and grinned.

Before Hickox met Rockefeller, he had seen the con man around Beacon Hill, usually talking with a group of people associated with the school that Rockefeller's daughter attended. "I had spotted him around the neighborhood. He's somewhat of a striking person with his unusual hue of orange hair and somewhat projecting eyes," Hickox told me. The memory seemed to have stayed with Hickox in part because of the people that Rockefeller was talking to. "There he'd be every day with a handful of Beacon Hill types who were familiar and prominent," Hickox told me. "I mean, really major figures."

A friend introduced the two men at a fundraiser at the Four Seasons, and they soon became friends. Over the years, Hickox would occasionally have doubts about Rockefeller's identity. But, all in all, Hickox didn't really question Rockefeller's story too much. After all, everyone else believed that Rockefeller was a Rockefeller. Plus, the con man was plainly charming. "There's a certain amount of mercurial skill with people that Rockefeller had," Hickox told me.

Hickox explained that when most people found out about Rockefeller's scam, they felt betrayed. They felt scared. But Hickox saw it all as an act, a sort of show.

"I was just thinking of that phrase from Tennyson's 'Ulysses,'" Hickox said. "Do you know that poem?"

I shook my head, mumbling something about maybe having read it in high school. Hickox explained that Tennyson's poem features the Greek king Ulysses, who wistfully remembers his early days as a warrior and wonders if he should set out on one last adventure. Hickox then quoted a few lines:

"All experience is an arch wherethrough
Gleams that untravelled world."

For Hickox, the relevance to our conversation was plain. Much like Alex Pentland, Tennyson argued that we are "a part of all that we have met," and by creating the fake Clark Rockefeller, Clark Rockefeller had become the real Clark Rockefeller, Hickox suggested. "In his mind, he is still Clark Rockefeller, even though he has been exposed. So much has been involved in this long evolution tested by experience," Hickox told me.

So Rockefeller was a Rockefeller because others believed that he was a Rockefeller. "So he created this network and just became a part of it?" I asked.

"That's right," Hickox replied. "And certainly he would have loved that way of looking at it."

When we talk about a con man like Clark Rockefeller, there's one final thing to think about: There's a little bit of a con man in all of us. Sometimes we do cheat and steal.[32] We are dishonest. In fact, you've probably already spun a few fibs today. "I'll see you at the party," you told a friend, even though you had no plans of attending the event. Or maybe you told your coworker, "I love your jacket," when in fact you believed the coat was painfully ugly. People will often tell as many as three lies during a coffee break–length conversation. This sort of deceit isn't limited to spinning fibs either. It turns out that there are even some people who lie for a living.

So how do we reconcile this fact — that most people are both trustworthy and untrustworthy? The question is important to understanding how we can improve our faith in others. There's a conflict here, to be sure. In his book *The Honest Truth About Dishonesty*, psychologist Dan Ariely argues that part of our nature is selfish.[33] Cash, fame, fancy houses — people desire it all. But at the same time, there's the issue of self-respect: Am I a good person? Am I kind and trustworthy? So when people do something that's wrong, they rationalize. Ariely puts it well: "Essentially, we cheat up to the level that allows us to retain our self-image as reasonably honest individuals."

This explains why it's often easy for people to lie and cheat: They don't see lying and cheating as lying and cheating. No doubt, people get nervous if they're spinning a clear and obvious falsehood. When people tell an unabashed lie, they become jittery. Their skin becomes clammy. They start breathing heavily.

But when we tell white, or social, lies, we often don't feel any anxiety at all. In fact, small embellishments can even have a positive psychological effect. College students who exaggerated their GPA in interviews later showed improvement in their grades. Their fiction, in other words, became self-fulfilling. "Exaggerators tend to be more confident and have higher goals for achievement," Richard Gramzow, a psychologist at the University of Southampton in England who ran the study, told me. "Positive biases about the self can be beneficial."

There's not much that separates a slight exaggeration from a massive whopper, though. When you're not telling the truth, you're telling a lie. These are all transgressions, big or small, and ultimately what we're doing is lying to ourselves. Dan Ariely once conducted a study that gives another way to understand this idea. For the experiment, he slipped into a college dorm and tucked a six-pack of Coke in half of the building's fridges. In the other fridges, Ariely placed a paper plate with a half dozen one-dollar bills.

As Ariely points out, if the students didn't care about what they were stealing — the Cokes or the money — both items would have disappeared from the fridge at the same rate. After all, if a student was really parched, he could have used one of the bills to buy a Coke. When Ariely returned a day and a half later, all the sodas had vanished. But the bills? No one had even fingered them. For Ariely, the point was that we don't like stealing things that have clear monetary value, like crisp dollar bills. But when we take a Coke from the fridge, we don't see that as, well, stealing.

There are many ways to shift this equation, as Ariely notes. We can make promises. We can clarify expectations. Studies also suggest that people are less trustworthy if they are anxious or stressed or just plain tired. Our connections to others matter, too, and we're more trustworthy if we know someone is watching. But perhaps most important, the research on lying makes clear that people rarely spin large yarns. In Ariely's experiments, for instance, very few people turned out to be dedicated wrongdoers. Almost no one in his studies fully took advantage of other people.

So why do we believe otherwise? Why do we think that others are so untrustworthy? Part of the issue is that negative events are often more salient in our minds, and so if something bad happens, we're more likely to remember it than something good. Another issue is the media. As a species, we didn't evolve to get a constant Twitter feed of negative news, and because of headlines that scream the news of one crisis after another, people believe that the world is far more cruelhearted than it really is. So while violent gun crime has been dropping steadily, most Americans believe that it's on the rise.[34]

As for Rockefeller, he and his daughter eventually made it down to Baltimore. Rockefeller had purchased a house not far from downtown, and he was in the process of building yet another persona for himself as Chip Smith. But a Baltimore realtor tipped off law enforcement, and the FBI soon arrested the con man. Later that day, two agents placed Rockefeller in a white-walled room to talk about his case.[35] The video of the interview is grainy and washed-out. It's hard to see facial expressions. The social cues are blurry and hard to read. But you can still see glimpses of the Rockefeller who convinced so many.

A few minutes into the video, one of the agents asks Rockefeller if he wants to tell his side of the story. Rockefeller looks the agent in the eye and then raps the table with his knuckles for emphasis. "My sincere apologies for the problems that I caused to you."

"Accepted," the agent mumbles with a wave of his hand. "We're all adults."

"My sincere apologies," Rockefeller says again.

Both of the agents nod their heads now.

"Thank you," one says. And for a short moment, Rockefeller's shoulders sink. He looks toward the table. A rapport had been established.

The agents, of course, didn't believe Rockefeller — he was the con man who proves the rule. Most people are worthy of our trust, and Rockefeller was eventually convicted of kidnapping and murder. And that bring us to our next chapter, which looks at how we can repair our faith once it's been broken.

Chapter 4

Can We Trust Again?

Learning from Rwanda

I N THE East African country of Rwanda, about twenty miles north of the capital of Kigali, Empimaque Semugabo went to go check on a pig. The animal lived in a small, mud-filled pen, and Semugabo pulled up some yam leaves to feed to the animal.[1] *Pigs eat a lot,* Semugabo told me as he pushed the large green leaves into the pen. Semugabo will eventually sell the pig at a local market, and the resulting profit will go to Semugabo — and some of the men who helped kill his family.

Two decades ago, a brutal genocide swept across Rwanda, and many of Semugabo's relatives died in the violence. Semugabo managed to escape, and today he often sees some of the men who participated in the murdering of his family. He will greet them with a warm handshake or a loose hug. They'll talk about their children or their crops or the latest development in soccer's Premier League, and for his part, Semugabo does his best not to think about how a group of men cast his family into a latrine to die.

Rwanda's genocide exploded in April 1994. After a gunman missiled down President Juvénal Habyarimana's plane, Hutu extremists rolled out an extermination campaign against the minority Tutsis.[2] The violence was fast and brutal and often executed by hand. Members of the Hutu militia hacked adults to death with machetes. They killed children by smashing their heads against a wall. The death toll eventually reached 800,000. "I cut down some alive and on their feet," recalled one killer who led a massacre in a church.[3] "I began to strike without seeing who it was, taking potluck with the crowd, so to speak. Our legs were much hampered by the crush, and our elbows kept bumping."

In hindsight, there aren't nearly enough reasons for all the murderous violence. Religion, language, and culture are all shared by both Hutus and Tutsis, and in many areas, the two groups lived together without incident for decades. Many intermarried and had families together. There were divisions along the lines of wealth and power, however, and for a long time Tutsis were the nation's elite. The group had more wealth, more education, more prestige. The Hutus had everything else, which wasn't very much. But in the early 1990s, a group of radical Hutus gained power, and they cultivated a sense of loathing. The Hutu leaders referred to Tutsis as "cockroaches." They blamed Tutsis for political instability. Anyone who worked with a Tutsi was a traitor.

About two weeks after the attack on Habyarimana's plane, some Tutsis ran into Empimaque Semugabo's village north of Kigali. They recounted how the Hutu militia had assaulted their village, burning houses, killing Tutsis, throwing grenades at anyone who tried to fight them. When Semugabo saw the victims, he was working in the fields. The morning was rainy and wet, and he knew there was no time to go home.

So he swam across a lake at the edge of the village and soon stumbled out of the water on the other side, tired and gasping for air. Looking back toward the village, he could see a group of men with machetes and sticks. He could hear their shouts echo over the water. Semugabo couldn't make out everything, but he watched as the men killed a small boy near the shore.

It was only later that Semugabo learned that the Hutu militia also attacked two of his sisters, three of his nieces, and his aunt on that morning. The men battered the women and children until they were dead or half-dead, and then they looted their houses. Another group of men hauled the corpses and barely breathing bodies to one of the village's outdoor latrines, a deep pit of feces and urine. The Hutus pushed the half-living tangle of arms and legs inside.

"There was no possibility of them escaping," one of the Hutus who participated in the murders recalled. "There was no human thinking."

On that morning, Semugabo fled north and joined the RPF, a Tutsi rebel group led by General Paul Kagame. Semugabo fought with the RPF for a while before moving to a village not far from where his family had been killed. Over the following years, Semugabo often saw some of the men who participated in the murder of his family. Some had gone to jail; others had done some form of community service. Many still lived in the area.

Eventually, after various efforts and initiatives and workshops, Semugabo began to reconcile with the killers, and today some of them work together in a small farming cooperative, sharing the profits from the animals that they raise. One of the men who participated in the killings is now the godfather to one of Semugabo's sons. "I trust them," Semugabo told me. "They also trust me."

How is this possible? You might believe that once trust is broken, it can never be repaired. This is the oft-repeated message of afternoon television talk shows, or as Dr. Phil says, "The best predictor of future behavior is past behavior."[4] But our faith in others can be restored. We are so deeply wired to work together that even after a terrible betrayal, we will place our faith in others again. In this chapter, I'll touch on why social trust goes wrong as well as examine some of the ways that we can rebuild our faith in others.

What's important to keep in mind is that while there's no question that Semugabo's act of forgiveness is remarkable, it's not as remarkable as people might believe. Many others have forgiven heinous crimes. In 1995, for instance, the daughter of Bud Welch died in the Oklahoma City blast.[5] At first, Welch wanted revenge, and he says that he would have murdered Timothy McVeigh himself if he had had the opportunity. But eventually Welch reconciled with McVeigh's family and even began advocating against his execution. Or take the case of Conor McBride.[6] In 2010, McBride shot and killed Ann Grosmaire. But Grosmaire's parents, Kate and Andy, ultimately forgave McBride, and during the judicial proceedings, the family argued for him to receive a lighter sentence. Even after the sentencing, the couple would visit him in prison once a month.

Not everyone is as forgiving as Semugabo or Welch or the Grosmaires. But most of us forgive all the time. We pardon friends who are late. We overlook colleagues who make rude remarks. We forgive for the simple reason that it rebuilds the bonds of the group.[7] Plus, sometimes we don't have much of a choice. To succeed at work, to succeed at home, to succeed at school, we have to work with others, and without some form of trust, cooperation is nearly impossible.

This sort of groupish pressure exists in Rwanda, largely due to its recent history. After most modern large-scale conflicts, the warring sides don't typically live together again in close proximity.[8] But the Rwandan experience is different, and many of the Tutsi families that fled to Uganda and the Congo during the genocide have since returned home to their old towns and villages. At the same time, many of the Hutus who participated in the genocide have finished their prison sentences and gone back to their old towns and villages. Today, Hutus and Tutsis, victims and killers, go to the same marketplaces. They work adjoining fields. They see each other at church and school and the local bar. They try to forgive for the reason that it makes it easier to work together again in a group.

Empimaque Semugabo and Seleman Jyamubandi had known each other for years before the genocide. Their cattle used to graze in the same valley, and for a long time the families of the two men lived on the same hill. Yet, in April 1994, Jyamubandi joined in on the attacks on the Tutsis. Area functionaries asked him to participate in the killings, and Jyamubandi got dressed in pants and a shirt and armed himself with a stick before meeting up with the Hutu militia.

"The genocide was planned by the local government officials," Jyamubandi said. "The government encouraged me." The officials assigned Jyamubandi to bring the bodies of the Tutsis to the latrine and push them into it — some were still conscious as they fell to the bottom. "If the people had been taken to a hospital, they could have survived," Jyamubandi said.

In the years immediately after the genocide, Semugabo avoided speaking with Jyamubandi. He thought that silence might be one of the best ways to make Jyamubandi regret what he did. But the two men eventually began a process of forgiveness. Semugabo wanted to move on, to give up his anger, so the two men participated in a workshop devoted to reconciliation, which "made the truth come out and the human side show up," Semugabo says.

The two men also held a small ceremony at Semugabo's house, where they drank beer and invited relatives to celebrate their coming together. During the ceremony, Jyamubandi promised that he would never let anyone hurt Semugabo's family again. Today, their wives belong to the same church. Their children attend the same school. Jyamubandi is one of Semugabo's closest friends. "I have dropped the anger and developed a human heart," Semugabo told me.

Bagwire Illuminee lives in Kigali. Her home is at the end of an alley, off a dirt road, not far from the city's downtown. When I drove up on a recent evening with my translator, a heavy mist hung in the air. City lights sparkled and shimmered in the distance. A few men sat around an outdoor bar watching a game of soccer on television. We hiked up a narrow street to Illuminee's house, past cement walls topped with barbed wire, past a woman cooking dinner on her stoop, past all the other houses packed into the hillside like so many office cubicles. By 8:45, we were in Illuminee's home, listening to the radio.

Every week, Illuminee follows the radio broadcast of the soap opera *Musekeweya,* which translates as "new dawn."[9] For a long time, some 90 percent of Rwandans followed the radio soap opera, with more than 60 percent saying that they listened to the show every week. Over the past few years, the program's numbers have slipped to around 85 percent, but even with the slightly lower listenership, the soap opera may still be one of the most followed radio programs in the world. It certainly is one of the most effective at promoting faith in others, and people who regularly listen to the show have a more positive view of trust.

On that spring evening, Illuminee had a half dozen people in her living room. A woman with a bright purple head scarf sat on a wooden sofa. A thin man with a baseball cap and watery eyes perched himself on a step. All were steadfast fans of the show, which revolves around two invented villages. The fictional towns are called Bumanzi and Muhumuro, and they each have their own hill and share a river that lies between them. Every season, the characters in the two villages fight and argue and feud but over time, they also forgive and placate and reunite. The show never explicitly mentions Hutus and Tutsis, and yet everyone who listens to the show knows what it's about, that the radio program is a metaphor for Rwandan society.

The narrative of the show is jumpy, with unexpected love affairs and cliff-hanger kidnappings. When I listened with Illuminee, the show first developed a plotline about a man who heard people throwing stones at his house in the middle of the night. Then there was a tender moment between a young woman and her male friend. In the final scene, a man visits his mother in prison. He tells her that a factory has been built. People's lives are improving. The villagers are coming together, he tells her. But his mother wants to hear none of it. "Remember we are always your family, so don't forget that," she tells her son.

The soap opera strives to be realistic. The program deals with some of the classic problems of Rwandan village life, like bad potato harvests, and to create believable dialogue, one of the show's writers hangs out in bars and listens to prostitutes talk up clients. But more than anything, the show gives people a way to start to make sense of the genocide. In many ways, this accounts for the soap opera's remarkable success, because to regain social trust, we first have to gain a sense of how our trust went wrong.

This is harder than it seems, and part of the issue is that too often confessions are non-confessions. Politicians, toddlers, steroid-juiced sports stars — all often admit fault without really admitting fault. When Pete Rose was the manager of the Cincinnati Reds, he often bet on baseball games, and the league eventually banned him from the sport because of his gambling. In his autobiography, Rose seems to want to come clean.[10] But he also brushes off his misconduct. He doesn't seem sincere. "I'm supposed to act all sorry or sad or guilty now that I've accepted that I've done something wrong," Rose writes. "But you see, I'm just not built that way."

What's important about confessions is that they give context, and in

Rwanda, people want to know what happened. They want to understand why the attacks occurred. A confession — or something more formal, like a truth and reconciliation commission — also typically addresses two related points. It underscores a sense of regret as well as offers some sort of commitment that things will not go wrong again. The Rwandan soap opera tries to address these issues, and the program relies on the work of psychologist Ervin Staub, who argues that genocide often requires "passive bystanders."[11] For Staub, people who remain quiet in the face of mass violence play a crucial role, and passive or inactive bystanders can give perpetrators a sort of tacit permission.

At the same time, the soap opera tries to show that people can adjust, that individuals can adapt, and over the course of the program, the biggest star of the drama goes from being the chief villain to the main hero. All of this works to promote a feeling of empowerment, a sense of understanding. Some years ago, psychologist Elizabeth Paluck conducted a study of the soap opera, showing that people who listened to the radio program were significantly more likely to believe that trust was a positive trait.[12] The listeners also reported having more empathy for others as well as being more open to dissent.

Before I left Illuminee's house that evening, I talked with the other dedicated soap opera listeners for a while. One man told me that the show inspired him to forgive the men who killed his parents. Another said that the soap opera helped her better grasp why people did what they did. No one argued that the show would fix all of their problems; there are some crimes that cannot be explained — or forgiven. Or as one man said, the soap opera might provide only 9 percent of the solution.

Instead, the soap opera seemed to give people a framework to begin to understand something that seems beyond understanding. "When a person is alone, it's very hard to imagine something different to make him happy and to mend his broken heart. That's why the program is an encouragement," Chantal Uwimbabazi told me. "It helps him or her gain that imagination."

One of the questions that haunts the soap opera — and Rwanda itself — is an enduring one: How could people have trusted so much?

Why didn't Tutsis and other Hutu moderates see the signs that a mass killing would occur? After all, there were all sorts of cues that genocide was imminent — in villages, in marketplaces, there was constant gossip about a coming attack. There had also been mass killings in 1959, 1963, and 1973, and in the weeks before the genocide, street gangs often strutted around Kigali, hailing the power of the Hutus. It all led one Belgian to observe that the Rwandan government "is planning the extermination of the Tutsi of Rwanda to resolve once and for all, in their own way, the ethnic problem."[13]

Let's first take a step back, though, because it turns out that our approach to risk — or our judgment of whom to trust — isn't totally logical. When you look at the data, it's actually pretty embarrassing. This goes well beyond the issue of mass killings, and we fear snakes more than cigarettes, even though snakes usually kill about a half dozen people a year.[14] Lung cancer, in contrast, kills more than 100,000 people annually. Or just look at sharks. If you watch a lot of TV, or even just follow Shark Week, you might believe that shark attacks have become an epidemic. But sharks kill only about four people a year, which is essentially nothing given the fact that about 200 million people visit beaches in the United States every year.[15]

The bottom line is that our approach to risk isn't always rational. If we were perfectly logical — if we could predict when a genocide was about to happen — our mental formula for risk should look something like this, according to writer Amanda Ripley, who smartly describes the psychology of risk in her book *The Unthinkable:*[16]

Risk = Probability × Consequence

But within our brains, our mental risk formula actually looks a lot more like this:

Risk = Probability × Consequence × Dread

The dread factor changes everything, and generally we dread things that have certain attributes. Gruesomeness, issues of control, uncertainty, graphicness — these all change the dread factor, as Ripley and other experts argue.[17] In her book, Ripley gives the example of airplanes. I'm often more afraid of snakes, honestly, so let's consider the reptiles again, because dread is what makes snakes appear more dangerous than lung cancer. Snakes seem like something that we can't control, as opposed to other risks such as smoking. Also, a snake attack appears uncertain. A Western rattler seems like something that could attack us at any time. And finally, a snakebite seems like a particularly graphic way to die.

The dread factor works against us in all sorts of ways. It makes us afraid of lots of things, people and situations that simply aren't that dangerous, such as sharks. Because of the dread factor, we're also scared of certain types of diseases — flesh-eating bacteria, for example — when all in all, they're actually pretty rare. But most relevant is the fact that dread makes us trust too much, and it was dread — or a lack of dread — that made hundreds of thousands of Tutsis stay when they really should have left.

Take the survivor of another genocide as an example. Elie Wiesel should be one of the least trusting people in the world. When he was fifteen, the Nazis sent him to Auschwitz.[18] At the Polish death camp, Wiesel watched babies being thrown into bonfires. He hungered constantly for something to eat. A dentist at the Nazi-run camp once pried a gold tooth from Wiesel's mouth with a spoon. "Here, there are no fathers, no brothers, no friends. Everyone lives and dies for himself alone," a Nazi guard told Wiesel. But Wiesel managed to survive, and he later described his story in the book *Night*, which helped him earn the Nobel Peace Prize.

Years later, a friend came to Wiesel and said, "Look, you work so hard. What are you doing with your money?"[19]

"Shares here and there," Wiesel replied.

The writer's interests lay in ethics, Wiesel explained; he didn't know that much about finance. So the friend introduced Wiesel to an investment manager named Bernie Madoff. To Wiesel, Madoff seemed impressive. The friend told Wiesel that the Nobel Prize winner was "not rich enough" to join Madoff's fund, but that Madoff would make an exception for Wiesel. "It was a myth that [Madoff] created around [himself]. That everything was so special, so unique, that it had to be secret," Wiesel once explained.

When Wiesel and Madoff got together for dinner, they didn't talk about finance. Instead, they talked ethics and education and whether or not Wiesel might resign from Boston University and teach instead at Queens College in New York City. The notion that Madoff was a fraud never seemed to have crossed Wiesel's mind. The writer eventually gave more than $15 million to the investor's fund, and once Madoff's Ponzi scheme was revealed, Wiesel lost it all.

"How did it happen? It's almost simplistic," Wiesel explained. "I have seen in my lifetime that the problem is when the imagination of the criminal precedes that of the innocent. And Madoff had imagination."

When it came to Madoff, Wiesel did not have a feeling of dread. He didn't see danger. It's not that the Holocaust survivor didn't know that people could be evil. Instead, it seems that Madoff's fund didn't engage Wiesel's sense of worry. The fund didn't seem uncertain or gruesome or something he couldn't control, and so Wiesel handed over his money. "We gave him everything, we thought he was God," Wiesel recalled. "We trusted everything in his hands."

If Wiesel didn't have dread, if he didn't mistrust, it's easy to see why so many of the Tutsis did not flee the country. At the time that the violence first broke out in 1994, many Tutsis simply didn't believe that their neighbors and friends and colleagues would all turn against them. The Hutus had the advantage of what Wiesel calls the "imagination of the criminal." But there's another set of questions that are just as important: Why did the killers do what they did? Why did the Hutus murder with such ease? How can people commit genocide?

In Rwanda, what's striking is just how personal the killings were, and many of the Hutu killers knew their victims well. One man told me that he killed a half dozen people who had lived in his village. Other victims explained how their friends and neighbors attacked them. Or recall Seleman Jyamubandi — he had been friendly with Empimaque Semugabo since Semugabo was a child.

How is this possible? The radio soap opera provided some glimpses of an answer, but there's more going on here, and when we think about trusting too much, we have to consider the incredible power of peer pressure. We typically associate peer pressure — and its cognitive kin, conformity — with teenagers. When it comes to smoking or teen sex or driving drunk, high schoolers seem particularly vulnerable to the opinions of others. But for most adults, our willingness to go along with the group is far stronger than we'd like to admit, and in a way, we're all constantly broadcasting our inclusion in a certain social group.

Consider, for instance, the clothes you're wearing today. Your decisions about your shoes (sneakers or loafers?) and rings (silver or gold?) and pants (khakis or jeans?) all underscore your desire to fit in.[20] They indicate what sort of group you belong to, what culture you want to conform to.

This pressure to conform, to go with the beliefs of the tribe, goes far beyond the issue of genocide. Almost every board of directors, almost every team of salespeople, suffers from this kind of social pressure in one form or another, and versions of the phenomenon have been behind the Enron scandal, the dot-com bubble, and the recent real estate bust.[21] In many ways, the issue is that people comfort themselves with the beliefs of others. As we saw with the research on the sociometers, people use their networks to support themselves.

When it comes to genocide, a lot of other factors are at play. When I spoke to psychologist Erwin Staub, who helped create the radio soap opera, he gave me a long list of factors that can build conditions for a mass killing: economic threats, uncertain futures, the dehumanization of others. In Rwanda, there was also significant violence leading up to the genocide, and that sort of brutal confusion can push people further into conformity. As Philip Zimbardo argues in his thoughtful book *The Lucifer Effect:* "Ordinary people, even good ones, can be seduced, recruited, initiated into behaving in evil ways under the sway of powerful systematic and situational forces."[22]

But perhaps what's most disconcerting is that groups do more than silence people's doubts. They might actually make people see things differently. Seleman Jyamubandi, then, may not have suppressed doubts when he threw the bodies into the pit toilet during the genocide. As Jyamubandi stood in the rain and mud, as he tossed the corpses into the latrine, as he watched the looting, he just may not have had any doubts at all.

A few years ago, Emory University psychologist Gregory Berns scanned people's brains while they were exposed to a type of peer pressure.[23] Not surprisingly, a large percentage of the subjects gave the wrong answer if they were told that everyone else gave the wrong answer. Berns, simply put, showed that peer pressure is a strong social force.

What was surprising were the brain scans. Because when Berns examined the data from the fMRI, he found that when people decided to follow the decision of the group, there was almost no neural activity, indicating that they were overruling their visual observations. Instead, the brain areas associated with emotional processing lit up, as if people were attempting to understand the social implications of going along with the group. While the study is far from conclusive, Berns argues that the pressure for conformity actually changed what people saw. "We like to think that seeing is believing," Berns told a *New York Times* reporter.[24] But the study's findings suggest that "seeing is believing what the group tells you to believe."

There are a lot of reasons to worry about the power of groups. But when it comes to social trust, perhaps the most disturbing thing is just how quickly these groups form. For the slightest, most irrelevant of reasons, we will discriminate against people outside of our clan. In Rwanda, radio programs were key in hardening the social lines between Hutus and Tutsis, and in the months before the killings, one radio station called RTLM made incessant calls for genocide: "Cut the tall trees. Clean your neighborhood," the announcer would say.[25]

The radio program mixed its genocidal messages with popular music and easy banter. It made it seem like being a proud Hutu was the thing to do. What's more, RTLM played its message over and over again; it reminded Hutus again and again that they should take action, later even giving very specific directions about whom to attack. To create the conditions necessary for genocide, this sort of propaganda is crucial. It builds up a type of social pressure for killing. It makes it seem like the killings are inevitable, and today many of the Hutu killers blame the radio station for the murders. Seleman Jyamubandi, for instance, told me that it was the RTLM radio program that inspired him to take part in the massacre. "It called for the Tutsi killing," he told me.

This might seem like a cop-out answer but it's not. Because even without the pressure of propaganda, we all have a deep propensity toward stereotyping. In many ways, this idea first took shape with another genocide survivor, psychologist Henri Tajfel. When World War II broke out in 1939, Tajfel was studying chemistry in Paris.[26] He had grown up in Poland in a Jewish family, and he managed to spend the war in a POW camp. But when Tajfel returned to Paris in 1945, his family was gone. Almost everyone he knew before the war was dead. Tajfel soon began studying social psychology, and in a way, his research questions were obvious. Why do people discriminate? How does genocide happen?

In one of his earliest experiments, Tajfel told a group of young men that he was administering a quiz that would test their visual skills.[27] Tajfel had the men estimate the number of dots on a page, then sorted the group into two teams based on their results. The distinction between the two teams was "flimsy and unimportant" according to Tajfel. But still, when he told the young men to divvy up some money among themselves, they gave more cash to the men on their own team.

The issue is that people outside of our clan appear less trustworthy, so we're less likely to put our faith in them. We view them as outsiders, as interlopers, and even something as arbitrary as the shape of someone's nose or the arch of his eyebrow or the number of dots that he estimates on a page can make it seem as if someone is not part of our group and thus less reliable and honest.[28] But the second and perhaps more important lesson is that it's easy to get caught up in our trusting ways. We can have too much faith. Or as physicist Richard Feynman once said, "The first principle is that you must not fool yourself, and you are the easiest person to fool."[29]

There are some solutions to trusting too much. One thing that's particularly powerful is dissent, as we saw in the radio soap opera. Active bystanders can play an important role in making sure that people don't trust too much. The good news is that a small amount of dissent goes a long way, as James Surowiecki argues in his marvelous book *The Wisdom of Crowds,* and often just one individual is enough to upend the power of conformity.

For example, in Philip Zimbardo's infamous Stanford Prison Experiment, an outsider — psychologist Christina Maslach — saw the guards abusing the prisoners, and she told Zimbardo that the experiment needed to end. In Solomon Asch's well-known conformity experiment, the presence of a single objector pulled down the effect of peer pressure by a third, as Surowiecki notes. The ability to empathize makes a difference, too, and in Stanley Milgram's conformity experiments, subjects were less likely to obey if they were sitting closer to the person getting the electrical shocks.[30]

Or take Paul Rusesabagina, who saved the lives of more than 1,000 people during the Rwandan genocide. His story was chronicled in a Hollywood blockbuster, *Hotel Rwanda.* Rusesabagina argues that he was just a regular guy who took action because he had no choice. But dig into his autobiography, *An Ordinary Man,* and it's clear that Rusesabagina had an outsider's sense of perspective. He didn't, for instance, have a strong allegiance to either Hutus or Tutsis, and it turns out that his father was a Hutu, his mother a Tutsi. Rusesabagina was also the manager of a large hotel in downtown Kigali, and it seems that he had constant interactions with foreigners.

But perhaps just as significant, Rusesabagina had a sense of empathy. He was someone who understood the power of connection. Take, for instance, how Rusesabagina describes making a business deal. "The very act of negotiation makes it difficult, if not impossible, to dehumanize the person across the table from you," he writes in his autobiography. "You are forced to make a compromise, and by doing this you are forced to understand, and even sympathize with, the other person's position." The takeaway, then, isn't that we need to deny all of our faith in others, or that we need to ignore our social nature. It is, after all, part of who we are. Instead, we need to make sure that we engage outsiders, that we promote dissent, that we don't become too wrapped up in our trusting ways.

Even with all this context, it remains difficult to comprehend the brutal depths of the Rwandan genocide. At one memorial site a few miles outside of the capital, I saw the skeleton of a woman who had had a wooden spike inserted into her vagina and driven through her body. At other sites, men hacked off the feet of small children. One group of killers pulled the hearts out of victims' bodies and ate them. Put simply, there was little dissent in Rwanda. Few were able to push back against the Hutu government, and through a dedicated and targeted approach, a small faction of government officials managed to turn a group of Hutus into monsters.

But people did survive the genocide. A nation still exists today. Every day in Rwanda, people are trying to live their lives. They send their kids to school. They ride the bus to work. Empimaque Semugabo now works as a security guard. Another victim that I spoke to runs a small milk company. Another survivor earns his income in home construction. And like people everywhere, they dream of a better society, of better opportunities. But for that to happen, there needs to be some sense that a massive break in trustworthiness has deep consequences.

When it comes to a small break in trust, punishment isn't all that important. When the transgression is small, a confession can seem like a form of atonement. But when the crime is large — a vicious rape, a brutal murder, a case of genocide — people need more. We want reparation and atonement, retribution and punishment. What's more, justice can work to create a sense of trust, a feeling of togetherness.

Rwanda struggled with this idea after the genocide. How does a nation provide redress to victims after a mass murder? What's the proper punishment for someone who hacks off the feet of a child? How could the nation create justice without leading to more killings? The nation's leaders also wanted the judicial process to empower the victims, and the government eventually decided to prosecute all of the perpetrators using a grassroots, mediation-style judicial approach. The system was called *gacaca,* which translates roughly as "on the grass," and it incorporated many of the nation's precolonial legal traditions, where a town elder would typically moderate a dispute between two villagers.

The *gacaca* process was remarkably decentralized, and each community essentially created its own genocide court. Individuals brought forward their own charges. Defendants argued their own sides. No lawyers helped the perpetrators or the victims, and many of the judges didn't have a legal background. Some worked as cooks. Others were farmers.

Without question, this sort of community-based approach comes with its own set of problems. Some Hutus didn't feel that the local judges were impartial.[31] Others didn't testify because they were afraid of retribution. One Tutsi woman claimed that her uncle would give her a cow if she falsely accused a man of rape. But overall, the *gacaca* system worked far better than you might expect. The process appeared to be relatively fair, and many Hutus were exonerated, with an acquittal rate of around 25 percent.[32]

At the same time, many victims said that the process gave them a sense of agency. By creating their own courts, by describing what had happened in front of the killers, many Tutsis began to nurture a sort of ownership over the genocide, according to political scientist Phil Clark.[33] What might be the most surprising is that the *gacaca* also provided a type of intimate liability for those who killed, and by confessing in front of their victims, many Hutus felt "a sense of release from feelings of shame," according to Clark. The Hutus were able to engage the people that they harmed. They could speak of their crimes — and ask for a way to work together again.

This social approach to justice matters more than you might think. It turns out that there's a groupish angle to the law, and when a trial is well executed, it can give people a broader feeling of dignity. If you're still skeptical, consider what happened in South Africa's Robben Island prison in the 1960s. Even by the standards of the Afrikaner-led government, the prison was a brutal place, as Chuck Korr and Marvin Close make clear in their book *More Than Just a Game.*[34] The men would have to hammer rocks into smaller rocks. Food was typically a filthy gruel. Some, like Nelson Mandela, ended up spending almost two decades in the prison, and the guards often brutally beat the men, telling them, "Here you will die."[35]

But with the help of the Red Cross, the prisoners eventually won the right to play soccer games on Saturday afternoons. The men dubbed the league the Makana Football Association, and they took the rules of the game very seriously. Everything was done according to FIFA rules — the club system, the number of referees, the way that complaints were registered. If a player had a dispute, he could turn to the Makana Football Association's disciplinary committee as well as a special appeals tribunal, according to Korr and Close. One quarrel over a disputed game dragged on for months, complete with legal briefs citing the Magna Carta. The referees' union even had a motto: "Service before self."

Why did the players take the game so seriously? Why, in a prison where the men could barely get a piece of food, would they take the time to establish a court to decide the implications of a bad offside call? I asked the question of Marcus Solomon. In 1964, Solomon had been picked up by the South African police while he was driving to a fundraiser with Winnie Mandela, and during his ten years in Robben Island prison, he became one of the soccer league's main administrators. Solomon explained that the game was a way for the men to build a sense of identity, a way of developing their shared values, an approach that brought them together as a community. "Sports developed out of our struggles," Solomon told me.

The league also gave the men a way to practice building a new type of nation. The prisoners were ultimately preparing for the day when they would take over South Africa. Take Dikgang Moseneke. He wrote his first legal brief as the prosecutor of the soccer league's appeals tribunal, and after the fall of the apartheid government in 1994, Moseneke became a judge on South Africa's Constitutional Court. Or consider Jacob Zuma. He was both a player and a soccer club administrator at the island jail, and he eventually became the president of South Africa in 2009.

Everyone on the island knew that the men were doing more than just kicking a ball around, including the prison guards, who eventually built a wall so that Nelson Mandela could not watch the games from the window of his cell.[36] "Our sports have played no small role in bringing us closer together," Solomon once wrote to his teammates.[37] "Some of us might say: Noble ideals and big talk which has no bearing on the real situation. My reply to those people is in the form of a question: If we had no noble ideals, would we have been here today?"

We often think that courts are only about outcomes: Did you win or lose? But it's not quite that simple, as psychologist Tom Tyler has argued. We also want our voices to be heard. We want people to respect our values. When researchers in Minnesota studied the experiences of drug offenders some years ago, they found that the convicts who believed their case was "handled justly" were more likely to finish a drug rehab program.[38] So if a cocaine addict thought that the judge was impartial, he or she was less likely to do cocaine again. And one of the main reasons that the convicts gave for staying off drugs was not the threat of more jail time or random urine testing or the promise of job training. It was meeting with the judge.

As for Rwanda, *gacaca* is over, and the process didn't heal all of the nation's wounds by any means. But for many people, the court system made a significant difference. I met Fredrik Kazigwemo one afternoon in a village devoted to reconciliation a few miles west of Kigali.[39] Short and thick, with the shoulders of a hockey linesman, Kazigwemo told me without emotion that he had murdered seven people during the genocide. Some died in their homes. A few were finished off in their fields. After the genocide, Kazigwemo went through *gacaca*. He also approached the families of the people that he had killed to ask for their forgiveness.[40] He explained himself in letters and personally visited their homes, and as he told me his account, our eyes met. He didn't seem worried or anxious or scared. Kazigwemo knew, it seemed, why justice was necessary.

For the past few years, Benjamin Ndizeye has been traveling around Rwanda, working with different communities to build up a sense of society, a feeling that other people can be trusted. Typically, a local pastor or village official will call Ndizeye and say there are people in his community looking to reconcile. Ndizeye will then spend a few days in the town, walking the group through a workshop built around a film called *As We Forgive*. Afterward, he'll typically help the group set up a small cooperative, which pools money so that the members can buy farmland or animals together.

While I was in Rwanda, I followed Ndizeye around for a while. We spoke with some of the survivors of the genocide. We visited some of the fields that the Hutus and Tutsis had planted together. Near the end of my visit, a Tutsi victim, Anastase Kayisire, told me that he believed that a Hutu woman in his cooperative may have lied about her family's role in the genocide. Had her husband really not participated in the murdering of his family? Had she really tried to protect his sister from the militias? He wasn't sure. "The truth is few," Kayisire told me.

It can be easy to understand some of the contextual factors that set the stage for a genocide. It can be easy, too, to watch someone do penance and serve time in prison. What's often the most difficult is building up trust again. To put it another way, a lot of trust recovery boils down to the question: Can people change? Because once we deal with our own disappointment, what makes a difference is that we will not be disappointed again. We're willing to trust people again, even strangers, but only if that trust is rewarded.

This makes our belief about the nature of the violation important. A few years ago psychologist Peter Kim gathered a group of subjects and showed them a video of an accountant applying for a job.[41] The subjects then found out that the applicant had once sent in a false tax return. Half of the subjects were told that the applicant's error was a matter of skill: The applicant did not understand the tax code well enough. The other half were told that the applicant's error was a matter of morals: The candidate filed the wrong tax return on purpose.

What Kim found was that the framing, or context, of the betrayal made a difference. If someone made a skill-based violation, an apology helped people trust that person again. But if someone made a moral violation, people became less forgiving. Why does this happen? According to Kim, we care about the nature of the violation because it suggests whether or not someone will double-cross us again. So if an accountant goofs up someone's taxes because he doesn't know the ins and outs of capital gains taxes, he may simply need more training. But if an accountant makes a mistake because he's morally corrupt, he's probably going to commit that same error again.

This issue goes beyond trust recovery. Stanford University psychologist Carol Dweck studies why some people regain trust, and for her, much of it boils down to the way in which we view human nature.[42] Some people, Dweck argues, have a "fixed" mind-set. They believe that either people have a talent, or they don't. Other people have a "growth" mind-set. For them, people can change. They can develop and improve.

In one now famous study, Dweck gave two groups of students some problems from an IQ test. After the exam, she lauded some of the kids in a way that emphasized a type of fixed mind-set, while the second group got kudos for their academic growth. And though the difference was nothing more than a matter of emphasis, Dweck found enormous differences in how the students approached future problems. Kids applauded for their raw intelligence faltered when the problems got more difficult. But that didn't happen to the children who received compliments for their effort or growth, and even when the problems became far more difficult, those students stayed engaged.

Dweck sees similar issues within relationships. Some people have a fixed mind-set toward others. They see any sort of betrayal as a deep-rooted flaw in the other person's character. They believe that any hint of trouble is a sign of the end. *Maybe it wasn't ever supposed to work,* they think to themselves, and then, like children praised for their intelligence, they stop working at the relationship. But people with a growth mind-set are different. For them relationships are a matter of understanding and learning. They believe that people can change, that betrayals can be forgiven, that trust can be recovered. Or as Dweck writes, "There are no great relationships without conflicts and problems along the way."[43]

Within this context, any effort to rebuild social trust in Rwanda is extraordinarily difficult, and in many cases it might be impossible. After all, no matter how the issue is framed, some Hutus committed deep moral violations, and even with a growth mind-set, it's impossible to excuse the atrocities. But still, hope remains. Just look at Ndizeye. One afternoon, he told me how a group of Hutus attacked his family shortly before the genocide began. He was a young boy at the time, eleven years old. His family was living in the Congo, just over the border from Rwanda, and a man came up to his mother with a spear, saying: "I want to kill you."

Ndizeye's family managed to escape, but they lost everything — their home, their cattle, their restaurant. Over the years, Ndizeye has worked to give up his sense of anger, his feeling of betrayal. Given the nature of Rwandan society, he engages with Hutus constantly. Most of them aren't perpetrators of the genocide. Rather, they're the children or the wives or the distant cousins of someone who killed. And it's here that Ndizeye — and the nation — might have the greatest reason for optimism, because the children or the wives or the distant cousins of someone who killed didn't commit a moral violation. Strictly speaking, they might not have committed any violation at all, and so a sense of trust can come more easily.

There is another takeaway, and that's that rebuilding trust requires some trust, and for Ndizeye, that's why the farming cooperatives are so crucial: They give people the chance to work together again. Within the cooperatives, Hutus and Tutsis can build a sense of reciprocity. They can engage in an extended exchange of tit for tat, and from that experience, Ndizeye hopes that a deeper culture of trust will arise.

In Semugabo's cooperative a few miles north of Kigali, each family donates around a dollar per month to the association, which is a significant amount of money in a place where most people live on less than two dollars a day. But even with all the community-building efforts, there are no guarantees. When I was in Rwanda, I asked Semugabo how long his cooperative would last. We were in a small sedan at the time, bouncing along a dirt road, driving Semugabo to his part-time job. He was quiet for a moment. The red-brown hills jumped and jangled outside the car window. He thought it might be around five years, he told me. But Semugabo didn't seem too worried about it. "Everything has a beginning and has an end. But now we choose to begin."

Semugabo's experience underscores the fact that we instinctively trust others, and there are clear signs that Rwanda has come back together. The country has one of the world's fastest-growing economies.[44] Starbucks now snatches up a quarter of their coffee exports.[45] Corruption — widespread elsewhere in Africa — is relatively low, and a few years ago, the Clinton Foundation gave President Paul Kagame its Global Citizen Award.[46]

But the Kagame regime also has a somewhat authoritarian soul, and within the public sphere, there's little room to express opinions that are contrary to the government's views. "There's freedom of speech. There's just no freedom after speech," one Rwandan told me. The Kagame-led government has also imprisoned opposition leaders and crushed independent voices for reform. Critics of the government have been shot and killed, while hundreds have been shipped off to "rehabilitation" camps.[47] For the international community, however, the last straw was Kagame's support of M23, a brutal rebel group in the Congo, and some nations, including the United States, have either slowed or stopped giving aid to the country.

But the more serious problems may be at the local level. The genocide still lurks behind almost every interaction, even if it's not always spoken about explicitly, as Jean Hatzfeld makes clear in his haunting book *The Antelope's Strategy*.[48] "At the market, we sell to one another without a qualm. In the [bars], we talk with them about farming, the weather, reconciliation; we share bottles and we exchange civil words of agreement . . . except about *that*," a Tutsi man told Hatzfeld.

For most Rwandans, trust remains a very fragile process, and it will probably stay that way for decades. Survivors have seen how uncertain the world can be, and even those who say they've reconciled still feel aggrieved. At the same time, Rwanda's leaders will also need to make a crucial decision. Does the government want to create the type of culture that sustains trust in the long run? Or will the authorities continue to stifle free speech, limit individual rights, and squash efforts at democracy?

The issue is obvious: While the nation's current authoritarian approach may create stability in the short term, it ultimately works to erode our faith in others, and the nation will need to empower citizens, embrace dissent, and foster civic equality if it wants to build this sort of faith in others. This is particularly important when it comes to creating faith across social lines. A few years ago, some sociologists conducted a study looking at the impact of growing social diversity in Canada.[49] They wanted to know if a greater racial and ethnic mix eroded our faith in others, and they found that by itself, diversity did not make people less trusting. Instead, there were two things that actually weakened trust: increased diversity and people connecting less frequently with their neighbors. What ultimately worked to erode people's faith in others, then, was a matter of feeling different — and isolated.

Plus, sanctions can misfire. They can smother our cooperative nature, and authoritarian governments can make us less trusting. They can snuff out our social ways. In a way, every parent knows this problem. Imagine, for example, you have a teenage daughter who generally takes out the trash.⁵⁰ But then one day you decide to start forcing your daughter to haul the garbage bags down the driveway. The issue is that your daughter will probably not want to take the bags out on her own anymore. Her social motivation (taking out the trash because of her ties to the family) has become replaced by external motivation (taking out the garbage because you tell her to).

In the end, our faith in others is something that comes from society's deepest cultural roots, and in the next section of the book, we'll look at some more specific examples of ways that we can promote social trust. As for Rwanda, there is reason to believe that it will eventually be healed. No one knows for sure, and while I was there, it did seem on occasion as if the nation's efforts at rebuilding trust were some sort of show, a type of fiction put on for visiting foreigners.

When I talked with killer Fredrik Kazigwemo, for instance, I felt at times like there was something manufactured about it all. His heartfelt talk of community, the search for forgiveness, the need for repentance — perhaps it was all staged? The thought tugged and nagged, and after the interview with Kazigwemo was over, I stepped outside into the bright afternoon sunshine. I took some pictures and chatted with some of the children, and as I stood there, I saw Kazigwemo walking with a Tutsi man who worked with the village. The two men couldn't see me, but I could see them, and they were holding hands.

PART II

How We Can Improve Trust

Chapter 5

Teams

"Go on Faith and Knowledge"

T H E first football game took place on November 6, 1869, when Rutgers University beat Princeton 6 to 4.[1] The game was different back then. Players couldn't actually run with the ball. They could only kick or hit it. Tackling wasn't as sophisticated either, and players would sometimes just throw themselves at each other in flying formations. Over time the game evolved. The rules were changed. New positions were added.

But for decades the sport emphasized strength over teamwork, and for many, the game remained a sort of organized mayhem. Give a player some instructions on where to go and when to do it, and if he had the physical prowess — and the raw desire — he would make it happen. "Coaches who can outline plays on a blackboard are a dime a dozen," Vince Lombardi once explained.[2] "The ones who win get inside their player and motivate."

All of that ended with Bill Walsh. In the late 1970s, the coach of the San Francisco 49ers created a new way of playing football, one which required far more trust. In the past, quarterbacks would either opt for a bruising, rushing play, or wait in the pocket to launch long passes to an open receiver. But under Walsh, the 49ers developed a new type of offensive attack. Walsh claimed that he invented the approach for a Bengals quarterback named Virgil Carter, who couldn't throw very far.[3] To address Carter's liability, Walsh created crisp, timed passing plays, and Carter would throw the ball to a place just beyond the line of scrimmage, assuming that a receiver would be there to make the grab.

The approach became known as the West Coast Offense, and Walsh used the offensive system to build San Francisco into a football power-house that included five Super Bowl victories. Football pundits dubbed Walsh "the Genius," while players like Joe Montana and Steve Young became Hall of Famers. "The beauty of Bill's system was that there was always a place to go with the ball," Montana once explained.[4] "I was the mailman, just delivering people's mail, and there were all kinds of houses to go to."

Take, for instance, what's known to football obsessives as the Catch.[5] The play marked the start of Walsh's NFL reign — and it took place on January 10, 1982. San Francisco was playing Dallas at the time. Some sixty seconds remained on the scoreboard. The 49ers were just a half dozen yards from the end zone, and if they scored a touchdown and field goal, they'd be going to the Super Bowl.

The ball was snapped to Montana, and three Cowboys soon bar-reled down on the quarterback as he scampered toward the sideline. Montana then spotted wide receiver Dwight Clark moving across the back of the end zone, and he threw the football in a high, tight spiral.

One step, two steps, Clark launched into the air and snagged the ball. But here's what might be the most surprising thing about the play: It turned out that Clark couldn't even see Montana, and still he contin-ued his route, knowing that Montana would throw the ball if he was open. In this chapter, we're going to look at improving faith within small groups, because that's often what underlies social trust. When we learn the norms of reciprocity within a group, particularly a diverse group, we're more likely to trust more broadly.[6]

As for Walsh, he believed that the process of building cohesion on a team began with expectations, and the coach would provide all of his employees with a memo detailing his goals and assumptions.[7] In these missives, Walsh would describe proper staff attire ("shirttails in"). He would spell out how people should act ("your focus must be on doing things at the highest possible level"). He would delineate what sort of attitude people should have ("affirmative, constructive, positive").

Walsh gave these written lectures to everyone: players, coaches, even groundskeepers. The document for the team's secretaries covered two pages. "Your job is not civil service or even big corporate business," Walsh wrote in bullet seventeen. "We exist to support and field a football team."

These lists seem pedantic, and frankly they are pedantic. Walsh knew this. He understood, in other words, that culture was something that he ultimately could not control. It was something that happened among the players. It was something that occurred within the team itself. Of course, a coach could nurture certain norms. Walsh could try, for instance, to ensure that no one saw himself as more important than anyone else. He once chastised a coach for having a vanity plate on his red Corvette.[8]

But in the end, culture is a very human, very connective sort of tissue. It was something that Walsh could only try to foster. Coaches needed to connect with players. Players needed to connect with other players, and if people bickered, Walsh recommended that they grab a coffee and talk it out on their own.[9] Or take how Walsh approached team practice. During training sessions, Walsh didn't want full-contact tackles or blocks. He didn't want the men showing how tough or fast they were. Instead, Walsh wanted the team to focus on working together. He was one of the first coaches in the NFL to have players run through practices in just shorts and a T-shirt.[10]

In his book *The Score Takes Care of Itself,* Walsh describes how crucial it is for a team to build up a sense of trust. "Combat soldiers talk about whom they will die for. Who is it? It's those guys right next to them in the trench, not the fight song, the flag, or some general back at the Pentagon, but those guys who sacrifice and bleed right next to them," Walsh writes. "I nurtured a variation of that extreme attitude in our entire organization, most especially the players: 'You can't let your buddies down. Demand and expect sacrifice from yourself, and they'll do the same for you.'"

For years, Walsh made all of his staff work together in a crowded office in Redwood City, California.[11] He wanted everyone to be able to listen in on everyone else's calls. He argued that the small space fos-

tered communication, and later, when the team moved to a more spa-
cious facility, he worried about the lack of openness. He thought that
a "country club mentality" might erode the team's ability to discuss
important issues. "The minute there is a difficulty," Walsh once explained, "you have to be ready to attack the problem and find a way
to communicate about it without being difficult. It's part of building
leadership throughout the team . . . [Players] are always talking with
each other and always listening."[12]

Walsh's focus on communication was new. At the time, football
coaches were all about command-and-control authority. One of Vince
Lombardi's star players, defensive tackle Henry Jordan, once joked that
"when Coach Lombardi says, 'Sit down,' I don't look for a chair."[13] And
when someone asked Jordan if Lombardi treated his best players any
better, Jordan said, "No. He treats us all the same — like dogs." Walsh
took a different approach. He encouraged players to speak up. He
promoted collaboration. He saw communication as a way to promote
trust and community. The 49ers coach even put together some rules
on the best ways to foster dialogue. Walsh's first law? Be a great listener.
Walsh's second law? "When you're not listening, ask good questions."[14]

The problem is that communication is hard, and talking to someone
else doesn't mean that you'll become friends or teammates or protect
the quarterback on game day. When it comes to groups, though, the
even bigger problem is that communication needs to both build cohesion and promote dissent. Cohesive teams can become insular. They
can become too trusting, and, in some cases, communication can
make a person's views more extreme than they already are. In one experiment, a team of researchers had two groups of voters — a group of
liberals and a group of conservatives — go into separate rooms and talk
for a few hours about hot-button political issues, like affirmative action.[15] The effects were unmistakable: The discussion made each of the
groups more politically rabid. The "liberals became more liberal," the
researchers wrote, and the "conservatives became more conservative."

The takeaway here is that when it comes to small groups, the devil's advocate might not be much of a devil. Author James Surowiecki's
writings on teams inspired this chapter, and he argues that "one of the
most consistent findings from decades of small-group research is that

group deliberations are more successful when they have a clear agenda and when leaders take an active role in making sure that everyone gets a chance to speak."[16] What's important, as Surowiecki makes clear, is that group leaders listen to the people who are most likely to disagree. A crowd can become wise, then, but only if the crowd has a chance to speak. "The confrontation with a dissenting view, logically enough, forces the majority to interrogate its own positions more seriously," Surowiecki writes.

Bill Walsh worried about this issue a lot. Many of his plays were deeply complex. His offense depended on the receivers executing a play "down to the inch," and during practices, after games, and between quarters, Walsh wanted his players and coaches to speak up if they thought something wouldn't work. Would the opposing cornerback be too fast? Would the receiver not be able to spot the ball? Would the other team plan to run a different defensive formation? How should they respond to a new type of onside kick?

Walsh built an expectation that players and coaches should give him feedback. He wanted everyone to weigh in. "I tried to remove the fear factor from people's minds so they could feel comfortable opening their mouths," Walsh once explained in an interview.[17] People "have to be comfortable that they will not be ridiculed if they turn out to be mistaken or if their ideas are not directly in line with their superior's. That is where the breakthrough comes."

Walsh's other solution to the communication problem was simpler. It was a matter of more communication. So once a week, all of the team's coaches, along with Walsh, would eat lunch with the players in the locker room.[18] They would talk over tuna fish sandwiches and sodas. Walsh saw it all as a way to make sure that people across the team knew each other, that the defensive line wasn't isolated from the receivers or special teams squad. "The person most familiar with a topic — you, for example — can get myopic, in need of an outside perspective," Walsh once wrote. And you can "learn a lot while eating your sandwich."

In the late 1960s, Bill Walsh worked as an assistant coach to Paul Brown of the Cincinnati Bengals. During the games, Walsh would sit up in a booth above the field and recommend to Brown which plays to run.[19] But as the head coach, Paul Brown wanted it to look as if he were the one actually figuring out if the team would go for a short throw or a strong-side run. For Brown's ego, for his sense of control, for the crowds that filled the stadium, he wanted to be seen as the man calling the shots. So Walsh would have to phone the play to an assistant coach down on the field. That assistant coach would then run over and give Walsh's decision to Brown, and Brown would grab a player and inform him of the play. The process was slow and laborious, and it taught Walsh a key lesson for building faith within teams: "Share the glory."[20]

In a way, the issue is a matter of fairness: If we work with others, we want a share of the spoils. Plus, the cold logic of the Prisoner's Dilemma haunts every cooperative activity. When it comes to a team, each individual is constantly faced with a choice: Do I betray the other person for a short-term gain? Or do I work with others for a long-term profit? Or consider an NFL wide receiver: During practice, should he run faster, or ask his quarterback to throw better? During a game, should the receiver take the time to congratulate the quarterback, or get himself a quick moment's rest? During the postgame interview, should the receiver give credit to his teammates, or should he take the glory for himself?

The issue is that if people are working for the good of the team, they want to know that everyone else is working for the good of the team. When other people trust, we're more likely to trust, and if someone feels like his contribution is not being valued, he's less likely to contribute. For leaders, though, there's a catch: If you value one person's contribution, you are not valuing someone else's contribution.

For Walsh, part of the solution to this problem was emphasizing the importance of the team. During team meetings, during games, and after practice, he constantly underscored the importance of the group. He didn't allow any post-touchdown dances.[21] There was no jeering at other teams. When Walsh saw a rookie hollering at a woman during training camp, he cut the man from the team.[22]

At the same time, Walsh worked to make sure each person was valued. He prohibited the bullying of rookies.[23] He recognized individuals. Yet he did so in a way that showed that it was all about the group's overall success. "The offensive team is not a country unto itself, nor is the defensive team or the special teams, staff, coaches, or anyone in the organization separate from the fate of the organization. We are united and fight as one; we win or lose as one," Walsh once wrote.[24] "Success belongs to everyone."

When it comes to teams, it's hard to understate the importance of Walsh's point about success belonging to everyone, and even the simplest of gestures — a word here, a pat on the shoulder there — makes a difference. They remind people that they're working together, that everyone is recognized. A few years ago psychologist Michael Kraus had a team of researchers categorize every single example of physical touch between players during a single NBA game.[25] If there was a fist bump or a head grab, Kraus's researchers made a note of it. Kraus then used the data to predict the team's performance, and he showed that if players touched others more frequently, they performed better both as individuals and as a team. "If I was a coach, I'd focus on starting a culture that is about these real sorts of cooperative actions," Kraus told me.

Trust, then, can become virtuous only if everyone gains. This matters for teams. This matters for society. But sometimes we need prompting. Sometimes that prompt can come in the form of a chest bump. Sometimes it can come in the form of a yell. Quarterback Steve Young was inducted into the National Football Hall of Fame some years ago, and during his acceptance speech he recalled some of his early days with the 49ers.[26] Young explained that when he first landed with San Francisco, he would not throw to a receiver unless he could see him.

After one of his first games, a coaching assistant named Mike Holmgren yelled at Young on the sidelines.

Wide receiver "Jerry [Rice was] open. Why didn't you throw it to him?" Holmgren called out.

"I couldn't see him," Young responded.

"Well, you better start seeing him," Holmgren replied.

At that moment, Young realized that the 49ers were a very different sort of football team. "Go on faith and knowledge," Young explained. "You can believe that I have learned that lesson many times."

Chapter 6

==========

The Economy

The Art of Trustworthiness

N ot long ago, Ray Young went to the U.S. post office in Silver Spring, Maryland. Young was sixty-seven years old with wide eyes and a thin mustache.[1] He had an artificial hip, and within a few months he would be walking with the help of a cane. On that July afternoon, Young parked his Toyota Corolla and stepped inside the post office. It was supposed to be like any visit to any suburban post office in any suburban town on any suburban afternoon: One or two postal workers behind the window. A steady hum of fluorescent light. The woody smell of paper. A long line of people that stretches six, seven, sometimes twelve deep.

Young took his place in the post office queue, according to a series of articles in the *Washington Post*. Earlier, another man — let's call him Jim — had mailed two envelopes. After Jim left, he realized that he should switch the delivery times of his envelopes, so he walked straight to the head of the line, skipping past all the other people in the queue. Young must have watched Jim and thought: *Outrageous. How selfish, how unfair. Who does that guy think he is, cutting the line like that?* So after Jim finished remailing his envelopes, Young waited for him in the vestibule of the post office, a small knife in his hand. The two men began brawling. Young pushed his knife into Jim's chest and shoulder before speeding off in his Toyota.

Psychologists describe Young's behavior as a type of "queue rage," and it happens more often than it should. A few years ago, a man in London killed another man after an argument over line jumping.[2] In Jacksonville, Florida, someone pulled a gun on a customer who had been "standing slightly off-center" in a line.[3] In Milwaukee, a woman slashed open another woman's nose because she had jumped into an express checkout lane with too many items.[4]

There's something extraordinarily petty about flying into a rage over line jumping, and there's no question that people who attack others over a spot in the express lane probably have deeper psychological issues. But at the same time, irritation over line jumping isn't all that unusual, and frankly, I suffer from a silent, nonviolent type of queue rage probably around once a year. Usually, it happens in my car. Traffic is backed up on a highway or bridge. Some car horns blare in the distance, and out of nowhere, a driver forces himself ahead of me. I glare and mutter and swear, simmering in frustration at the outrage.

A few years ago, the *New York Times* ran an article titled "Why Waiting Is Torture," and the piece gave an unambiguous explanation for queue rage: It's about fairness.[5] When someone cuts in front of us, it offends our sense of justice, and we're willing to go a long way to make sure that people who arrive later than us don't get served before us.

A few years ago, some Israeli researchers studied people's preferences for different types of lines, as the *New York Times* notes.[6] Would people rather stand in a first-come, first-served line? Or would they rather wait in a "multiple queue" line, which is common in supermarkets and requires individuals to wait in separate first-come, first-served lines? People overwhelmingly wanted their lines to be first-come, first-served, and they were willing to wait some 70 percent longer for this sort of justice. In other words, in exchange for their time, people got something that's often just as important: the principle of fair play.

In previous chapters, we've been looking at how and why we trust. In this chapter, we're going to look at our economy and what it means for our sense of society. Why? Well, it turns out that one of the causes of the nation's recent collapse in social trust has been the soaring rise in income disparity, and I hope to convince you that economic fairness works as a type of social trustworthiness. It supports a sense of community. In his provocative book *The Penguin and the Leviathan,* Yochai Benkler writes thoughtfully about issues of fairness — Benkler's work inspired this chapter — and the Harvard law professor argues that notions of equity are crucial to any sort of cooperative system. Without some sense of fairness, we can't work together.

Or think of it this way: Because we're more cooperative than any other animal, it seems that we care more about fairness than any other animal, and our response to inequity is often a matter of unrestrained emotion. Scientists can see this in brain scans, and the brain region that's associated with processing feelings of disgust — the anterior insula — typically roars into action when someone sees or smells something foul. What's striking is that the anterior insula also kicks into gear when we experience inequity.[7] In other words, the same neurons fire when you see a cockroach on your bowl of cereal as when you see someone cutting you in line at the post office.

This doesn't always happen. Sometimes we can live with a little inequality. We will accept a lower salary for a job because we need the work. Or we will pay for something at a restaurant that we did not order because we don't want to make a scene. A few years ago, some scientists at the University of California, Los Angeles, studied the brains of two dozen subjects as they considered an unfair proposal.[8] And it turned out that when people agreed to an unfair deal, one of the brain circuits associated with self-control lit up, while the anterior insula — the area tied to disgust — became less active. As science writer Wray Herbert points out, our brains, it seems, can limit our emotional outrage in order to endure a bit of inequity. The acceptance of injustice, then, isn't an issue of greediness. Rather, it appears to be a matter of dialing down our sense of revulsion.

In Ovid's epic poem *Metamorphoses,* Ajax is a man of grit and strength, of muscle and devotion. He is the most athletic, most loyal soldier in the Greek army, and Ajax believes that because of his size and steadfastness, he deserves one of the most treasured prizes of the Trojan War, the precious armor of Achilles. The issue, as philosopher Paul Woodruff describes in his book *The Ajax Dilemma,* is that Ajax has to compete against Odysseus.[9] Wily and inventive, smart and slick, Odysseus is the man who figures out a way past both Scylla and Charybdis. Odysseus, then, is the charming brain to Ajax's loyal brawn, and he wants the precious armor, too.

King Agamemnon has Ajax and Odysseus each give a speech in front of a panel of judges, arguing his case. But it's already too late, according to Woodruff. In a battle of words, Ajax is doomed. He stands no chance, and the prize goes to the brainy Odysseus, while Ajax feels deeply betrayed. For years, Ajax has been a devoted warrior. He saved the life of the king. He once even rescued Odysseus from death. As Ovid writes, Ajax is "conquered by his sorrow," and the warrior eventually impales himself on his sword, killing himself.[10]

We live in a world of high-stakes competitions. Like Ajax and Odysseus, we compete for salaries, we compete for partners, we compete for friends. But landing the rewards — the money, the fame, the suits of armor — is often a tricky business. It would be nice, of course, for society to recognize the efforts of everyone equally. But we also want to highlight the aces, the top performers, the Odysseuses. And, by their nature, rewards are scarce.

On the one side, it's clear that Odysseus should win the armor. He is the inventive genius. His work is a matter of superior imagination, and without Odysseus's idea for the Trojan horse, the Greeks might still be laying siege to Troy. Still, when society's Ajaxes see the prizes always going to the Odysseuses, they feel hoodwinked, as Woodruff told me when I reached him in his office at the University of Texas. They've worked hard. They've been loyal. What's their reward? In the end, no system can function without an Ajax. He ensures that the work gets done. He sticks with you when times are tough. But as Woodruff told me, Ajax might be replaceable, but if you lose too many, an organization will fall apart.

Woodruff calls this the Ajax Dilemma, and the message is simple: Fairness alone isn't enough. Leaders also have to create a feeling of community, and that is where things went so wrong for Ajax. The contest between him and Odysseus was based on clear rules. Odysseus didn't cheat. Odysseus wasn't dishonest. But the process gave Ajax no meaningful way out, as Woodruff suggests. The loyal soldier had no way to feel pride, to feel part of something bigger, so he took his own life. "Justice is what ought to have kept Ajax on the team, or, more generally, justice is what ought to keep any community together through the stress of disputes," writes Woodruff.

What does this have to do with our economy? A lot, actually, because our financial system is a type of contest. It's a competitive market. But at the same time, our economy is built around the idea that everyone profits. This is true at the micro level. When you buy a carton of milk at the grocery store, you and the store benefit. The storeowner lands some revenue, while you get some tasty milk. This is also true within an organization: You go to work and earn a decent salary, while the company gains from your labor. Even at the macro level, our economy relies on the notion of mutual benefit, and countries with more equitable distributions of wealth have higher rates of economic growth.

What's more, fairness pays off when it comes to business. In the long run, firms gain when they're more trustworthy. I recently visited the headquarters of the natural beverage company Honest Tea and met with the firm's cofounder Seth Goldman. As Goldman explained, the company has long been dedicated to trustworthiness, and one of the reasons that Goldman called the firm Honest Tea was to underscore its commitment to probity. Or consider a sample line from the firm's original business plan: "We strive for relationships with our customers, employees, suppliers and stakeholders which are as healthy and honest as the tea we brew."

As Goldman and I sat in an office room, bottles of tea between us, he explained that shoppers are deeply aware of whether they're being treated fairly or not. In fact, even the slightest change in Honest Tea's product can catch the attention of consumers, and when the company recently made a very minor change to the design of its bottle — it put a larger dimple in the bottom — Goldman immediately heard from customers, who thought they were getting less tea for the same price.

The new bottle held the same amount of tea as before. It just looked like the bottle contained less tea. But still, Goldman took the concerns seriously, and the company began placing stickers on its bottles describing the change. "We clearly need to do a better job explaining why the bottle has this design," the firm noted at the time. "In the next label run we plan to say something to explain this to our customers. We hope that makes you feel that you can still trust us and will stick with us."

From an economic perspective, this sort of trustworthiness makes sense, because reliability is what turns a one-time interaction into a repeat interaction. If people think that they're overpaying for a bottle of tea, they're not going to want to buy that bottle of tea again. Same thing within a company. If your boss is a jerk — if he or she underpays you — then it's time to find new job. This also explains why studies show that more social cohesion leads to increased GDP: If we believe people are generally trustworthy, then we're more likely to engage them in trade.

The issue is that Honest Tea is unusual in its dedication to fairness. Once, while I was visiting Paul Zak in California, he and I drove to his lab on the Claremont campus, and as we sped along the highway, Zak argued that one of the main problems with business today is that firms don't do enough to inspire trustworthiness. Just look at television advertisements; most of the TV commercials today brim with half-truths. Or, as Zak told me, businesses often encourage people "to check your morality at the door. To check our social nature at the door."

Before Zak became fascinated by oxytocin, he edited a book called *Moral Markets*. The book is thick, some four hundred pages long, with chapters written by two Nobel Prize winners. It includes writings by many of the people that we've already met in this book, such as Frans de Waal and Robert Frank, and the book argues that moral values are what drive a market economy. Plus, ethical firms often do better in the long run: "Our research revealed that most economic exchange, whether with strangers or known individuals, relies on character values such as honesty, trust, reliability, and fairness."

But when it comes to the economy, fairness alone isn't enough. This goes back to the Ajax Dilemma: Communities often require competitions, while competitions often require a sense of community. In other words, business has a social side, and our economy should create a sense of togetherness. If we want both the Ajaxes and the Odysseuses on our team, if we want to keep a client or an employee, there needs to be a connection that extends beyond the economic exchange itself.

The research on oxytocin provides another way of understanding this idea, and according to Zak, markets can engage our hardwired bonding system in ways that make an economy more productive. When we're more empathetic, when we spark the social motivations of others, people act in more trusting and trustworthy ways, and thus create new opportunities for mutual gain. What's more, Zak argues that this sort of social connectedness is what produces wealth, and research by the neuroeconomist and others has shown that nations with deeper social bonds have more dynamic economies.

The key, it seems, is creating a business culture that supports our social nature. None of this is economic rocket science, to be sure. It's about relationships. It's about community. It's about purpose and values. What's new is that our emotionally driven faith in others can become a type of habit. Or recall the work of David Rand, who studied almost two thousand people playing the Prisoner's Dilemma. The results showed that if people saw a lot of collaborative behavior in their everyday lives, they became more instinctively trusting. Or as Rand and his colleagues argue, "intuition supports cooperation."

For a real-world example, let's take Honest Tea again. A few years ago, Coca-Cola purchased Honest Tea. The move angered many of the organic firm's customers, and Goldman responded quickly to the complaints, detailing why the move was good for the organic drink firm's mission. In his explanations, Goldman noted that what matters are values, and since the purchase Honest Tea has stuck to its ideals. For a while, Coca-Cola wanted Honest Tea to remove its "no high fructose corn syrup" text from its bottles. Honest Tea disagreed, and the labeling remains. What's more, the company has continued to build relationships, to create community, and sales remain strong. In other words, Honest Tea's customers may have learned something too, even the ones with the Honest Tea tattoos: Responsible businesses foster togetherness because when it comes to markets, we want a very different experience than Ajax, who says before he dies, "Now dishonored / Thus am I prostrate."[11]

A few years ago, Harvard University psychologist Michael Norton conducted a survey.[12] First, Norton asked people how wealth should be distributed in the United States. Overwhelmingly, respondents chose a fairly moderate distribution of wealth. In a perfect world, Americans thought that the top 20 percent of people should have around 35 percent of the wealth, while the bottom 20 percent should land about 10 percent. This alone is notable. The results were consistent across backgrounds, so whether the person was a Republican or Democrat, white or black, young or old, he or she wanted the nation to have a fairly equal distribution of riches. As Norton put it, most people wanted the range of American wealth to look like someplace in Scandinavia.

Norton then asked people what they thought the actual wealth distribution was in the United States, and that's where things started to get weird, because the actual levels of inequality and the expected levels of inequality were not even close. For instance, people guessed that, on average, the top 20 percent of Americans had around 60 percent of the wealth. But if wealth is defined as net worth, the top 20 percent of Americans actually own more than 85 percent of the total. In short, the survey suggested that Americans know that inequality exists in the United States; they just have no idea how much. And if you compare the current distribution against the desired distribution, the wealthiest Americans should have 50 percent less money.

Why does this happen? When I asked Michael Norton, he told me that the explanation is "pretty boring." The issue, Norton explained, is that we typically compare our wealth to the wealth of the people that we know well. So when a researcher asks us who has a lot of money, we think about the people who live in our neighborhood. But the people in our neighborhood are a particularly bad comparison group, since we tend to live with people who have similar levels of wealth. People who have lots of money tend to interact with other people who have lots of money, while people who live in poverty tend to interact with other people who live in poverty. This makes it hard to understand that some people may have a lot more — or a lot less — money than we do.

But the research is clear. Our middle class is shrinking. Social mobility is low, and in cities like New York, only 10 percent of kids who grow up in the bottom 5 percent of income reach the top 5 percent as adults.[13] More than that, the rate of poor kids becoming rich adults in the United States lags behind all sorts of nations, from Germany to Canada.[14] Among high-income democracies, in fact, only the United Kingdom shows worse economic mobility than the United States. At the same time, income inequality is growing, and in many cities the level of wealth disparity matches that of developing nations.[15] In Los Angeles, for instance, the level of inequity is now similar to that of the Dominican Republic; Chicago matches up with El Salvador; and New York City ranks up with Swaziland.

All in all, the data here are pretty ugly, and the growing equality gap is eroding our faith in others. It's tearing away at the sense of community that fuels our social ways, and some, like political scientist Eric Uslaner, argue that income inequality is almost entirely to blame for the recent dramatic fall in our faith in others.[16] Inequality, then, is not just a problem that threatens our economic system. It's a problem that threatens society itself. Think back to Ray Young, who got into a brawl at the post office. He saw Joe jump the queue, so he pulled out a knife. He was willing to stab someone in order to uphold a sense of equity. "I was fighting with a guy," Young told the police when they caught up with him. "He cut the line and I said something to him."

Chapter 7

Government

Trusting the Tax Man

U P UNTIL fairly recently, Somalia was, for all intents and purposes, without a central government. Over the past two decades, there have been state-building fits and starts, charters and constitutions, transitional governments and loose coalitions. But for the most part, there was no state. Warlords functioned as societal power brokers.[1] Sewer lines were rare. Hospitals seemed like a luxury. Education was limited, and today only a minority of Somalis know how to read and write. For a while, a provisional government issued passports, but few other nations recognized them. Transparency International recently ranked Somalia as one of the most corrupt nations in the world, which is saying a lot, given that the competitors are places that actually have governments.

When you think of Somalia, you might think of the pirates who have been hunting ships in the Arabian Sea or the incident in 1993 when American forces battled Islamic militia in the streets of Mogadishu. But the life of the people who actually live there is more along the lines of *MacGyver* meets East Africa. People are highly self-reliant. In the early 1990s, for instance, just as the government began to disintegrate, Mohamed Aden Guled decided to establish a newspaper in Mogadishu.[2] To communicate with his reporters, Guled would pay for time on a shortwave station. Because there wasn't a working mail or phone system, Guled had couriers who delivered copy for advertise-ments in person. Two gas generators powered his printers, since there was no electricity. What appeared to give Guled the most satisfaction, though, was the fact that he had 190 kids working as newspaper boys. "That's 190 boys with jobs," he told the *New Yorker*. "That's 190 boys not fighting."

We often overlook the role of government. There are the obvious services, of course, like supplying water and policing our borders. But nation-states also regulate building codes, secure debts, and invest in communication infrastructure such as cell phone towers. Govern-ments also go a long way to establish norms and values; they promote a sense of unity and culture and civil society. And to live in a country without a state is like living in the Middle Ages, except that the soldiers carry AK-47s instead of swords. In Somalia, seven roadblocks once dotted one of the city's main highways and each one was manned by a different armed group looking to collect a bribe.[3] To get through the "border crossings," either you paid a tax or you arrived at the road-block with your own contingent of armed men and fight-ready stares.

The lack of a state in Somalia did not mean the total collapse of so-ciety. We are, after all, a highly cooperative species, and in ways big and small, Somali life went on. In some areas, markets flourished. People continued to trade and grow crops and do business. A few years ago, a government managed to stagger its way out of the political chaos, and the nation now has a parliament and a president. Police walk the streets of Mogadishu. People can get electricity. But faith in the government remains tentative. The United Nations has already found evidence of massive corruption, and more than a dozen tax collectors have been murdered in recent years due in part to widespread skepticism about government initiatives.[4]

Political trust is different from social trust. Political trust measures our faith in government, and it is crucial for any large-scale commu-nity. More than two thousand years ago, Confucius argued that trust was more important for a leader than food or weapons. "If the people have no faith in their rulers, there is no standing for the state," he ex-plained. And for the most part, the philosopher's idea has held true, as scholar Onora O'Neill has argued.[5] In her work, O'Neill cites a few examples supporting Confucius's point, like the British government in World War II. I'll give a few more: despite chronic food shortages, the Communist government has stayed in power in North Korea. In Egypt, guns and truncheons and tear gas did little to stop the recent overthrow of dictator Hosni Mubarak.

In the United States, too, political trust has been in a steady nosedive. In 1958, 73 percent of Americans said that they "trusted the government in Washington."[6] In other words, people believed that government could execute, that politicians could solve pressing issues of public policy. But today only 19 percent of Americans trust Washington. Consider that statistic for a moment: More than 80 percent of Americans believe that the federal government is unreliable and untrustworthy.

This breakdown in political trust has all sorts of consequences. When I looked at data from the DDB's Life Style Study, provided by DDB Worldwide Communications Group, I found that political trust correlates with key social outcomes. If political trust is high, people typically earn more money and have more schooling. In areas with high political trust, there's also less crime and a larger proportion of people own their own homes. (For state-by-state snapshots of political and social trust see page 137.)

Low political trust also means low social trust, and the more that we have faith in our political leaders, the more that we're willing to place our faith in people we don't know. In a way, this goes back to Paris Hilton: Without a sense of order and safety, without a sense of rule of law, trust must be thick, and we trust only those we know well. But with institutions, with laws and cops and courts, trust can be thinner. We can trust strangers more easily. Or think of it this way: If people are often very trusting, then we need to do more to improve trustworthiness so that their trust is rewarded.[7]

But there's more at stake because governments also model trust — and trustworthiness — and when individuals see wasteful government agencies, they're less likely to place their faith in strangers. Plus, governments can promote a culture of empowerment, which makes it easier for people to trust others outside of their groups.[8] And finally there's the fact that government without some sort of political faith is powerless. Without some measure of faith, political leaders can't govern. Or just pick any of the most pressing issues facing the country today: the economy, terrorism, climate change. Each issue requires a coordinated approach. No local institution can tackle these issues. Not states, not your local town council.

The question then is: Can our trust in government be improved? How can we avoid devolving into some sort of dystopian, Somalia-like future?

At its core, government is a type of social contract, and in theory it works something like this: Individuals enter into an agreement, and in exchange for security and stability, they give up some of their freedom and liberty. Government, then, is when people consent to be governed, and in return they receive governance.

What this all means is that government needs to perform. It needs to produce benefits for the people being governed. This explains, for instance, why corruption has such a negative effect on political trust. When an official skims off the top, he is making government work for himself rather than for society as a whole. Local leaders often understand this idea well. They know that their jobs depend on delivery. Has the city put in a stop sign on Fifth and Vine? Have the trees on Center Street been trimmed? Did the fire truck arrive at the Saturday blaze fast enough?

Baltimore mayor William Donald Schaefer used to ride around the city at night looking for potholes.[9] He followed garbage trucks to find out why trash wasn't being picked up. "Do It Now" was Schaefer's motto, and when asked about his leadership style, Schaefer said simply: "Would you believe I have my nose in everything?"[10] The voters loved Schaefer for it, forgiving his wild temper (he would bawl out officials) and his spiteful side ("Dear Edit-turd" was how he once began a letter to a newspaper).[11]

Most of us don't think of government as an institution that needs to perform. Part of the issue is the shortsightedness of human nature. Government seems distant and institutional because it often is distant and institutional. So we may trust local government — we see someone picking up our trash each week — but the state or federal government that is hundreds or thousands of miles away? Not so much.

And then there's the fact that some agencies don't seem to actually believe that their job is about delivery. They don't track outcomes.[12] Ineffective programs aren't shut down. The consensus-building nature of the legislative process contributes to the issue, creating disparate and often uncoordinated programs. Today, for example, fifteen different federal agencies manage the nation's food safety program, operating under the jurisdiction of some thirty different laws.[13] Similar problems exist at the local level; when I looked at the return on investment of the country's school districts for the Center for American Progress, I found that low productivity costs the nation's school system as much as $175 billion a year, or about 1 percent of the country's gross domestic product.[14]

But when it comes to political trust, performance is crucial. It's the way that we know our trust is being reciprocated, and politicians who improve outcomes can do a lot to improve our faith in government. Look at what happened in Great Britain in the early 2000s.[15] At the time, it seemed as if the nation's public sector was falling apart. The police seemed flat-footed, and one woman had her house robbed three times over the course of two days.[16] The nation's famed rail system didn't seem so famed, and in the fall of 1999, thirty-one people died in a London train accident.

The situation was particularly embarrassing for Prime Minister Tony Blair. He had run on a good-government platform, and as he stumped around the country for his 2001 reelection campaign, he handed out "pledge cards" that listed his policy goals and how voters could hold him accountable. "When we make a promise, we must be sure we can keep it. That's page one, line one of a new [government] contract," Blair explained.[17]

Blair won reelection, and within weeks he decided on an approach to improving faith in government that at first glance seems childish: He created goals. Within health care, for instance, there would be a 40 percent drop in heart disease mortality. Every hospital would also have to ensure that no one waited longer than six months for non-emergency surgery. There would also be an increase in student test scores — and a measurable decrease in street crime.

Governments have long set targets, of course. That was far from novel. What was unusual about Blair's initiative was that the metrics were focused. Many of the reform areas had just a few goals, and some initiatives, such as reforming the railway system, had only one. Plus, Blair's targets were about engaging people and their experience of government. When it came to improving the performance of the rail system, the main target wasn't about maintenance or capital expenditures or new locomotives. It was about improving the punctuality of trains.

Over time, Blair's goals shifted the culture within agencies, and departments began writing out detailed plans, connecting their work to the outcomes set by Blair and his team. To build capacity, the prime minister also created a type of government performance SWAT team, which supported the reform efforts within the different ministries. The media began tracking the targets, and eventually the government showed success in almost every major area. In education, reading and math scores went up. In health care, waiting times fell. Street crime dropped off. "Blairism has restored faith in government as a creative and essentially benign force," one financial reporter wrote.[18]

Blair's effort did not tackle sweeping reforms. His initiative did not require major legislative changes or special commissions or high-profile committees. Nor did the work ultimately save the prime minister's legacy. In 2003, Blair supported President Bush's decision to invade Iraq, and many in Britain saw the decision as misguided. Hundreds of thousands of antiwar marchers flooded the streets of London. Faith in government again faltered — and for many Britons, Blair leaves a mixed legacy. But the point of Blair's reform efforts was not to save the prime minister from himself — or to save the nation from what many believed was an ill-conceived war. The point was to show that government can deliver.

If faith in government was all about performance, the world would have far more dictators. After all, almost every autocrat promises to make government stronger and more effective. Hitler, for example, murdered millions while his regime created the world's first nation-wide highway system. Italian dictator Benito Mussolini built a police state while making the trains run on time. President Vladimir Putin oversees a "soft authoritarian" regime built on the premise that Russia will devolve into instability without a strong leader.

The point is that our faith in government contains a contradiction. On the one hand, we want government to deliver. Alexander Hamilton referred to this idea as government's "energy," and he believed that this sort of vitality was one of the most important signs of a strong, trustworthy government.[19] On the other hand, we want government to be legitimate, to represent the majority of people, and we're reluctant to give too much power to a few. Political scientist Larry Diamond suggests that this is an unavoidable tension: We want government to perform, but no one wants to live in a police state.

The Founding Fathers understood this issue as well as anyone, and the framers of the Constitution baked accountability into the nature of American government. To create a system of checks and balances, the powers of the executive are separate from the powers of the legislature. Plus, as Americans, we have certain famously unalienable rights, like the right to liberty, and while these mechanisms make our government less effective, they also ensure that the nation will not easily devolve into tyranny.

The issue isn't that politicians are different from you or me. The issue is the caustic effects of power. A few years ago, psychologist Dana Carney had a group of subjects gather in a room.[20] Some of the subjects were told that they were leaders. Others were dubbed subordinates. Carney then hid a hundred-dollar bill among some books, and a computer told half the subjects to steal the money, while the other half were instructed not to. Then Carney asked the subjects to convince her that they did not pocket the cash.

The results? The people who believed that they were leaders had a much easier time spinning the truth. They fidgeted less. They spoke more eloquently. They had lower stress hormone levels. Power, it seemed, gave the subjects a type of emotional protection from the stress of lying. For them, rationalizations came much easier, and so they showed less anxiety about telling a fib.

The moral is not that power is bad. For a nation or a company or even a family to exist, someone needs to make decisions, and even in the most decentralized of groups, some people have more authority than others. But as psychologist Dacher Keltner has argued, power is a form of decay. It makes us less trustworthy. It pushes us to be less empathetic. For trust in government, the implications are obvious. Government should do what it says for the people that it represents, and we need to hold political leaders accountable. We need to create systems that ensure that political authority isn't abused. James Madison was right when he argued that "all men having power ought to be distrusted to a certain degree."[21] Now we just have the science to prove it.

When Ronald MacLean-Abaroa became the mayor of La Paz some years ago, he knew that he would uncover some corruption in city government. MacLean-Abaroa had grown up in the Bolivian city, and he had often heard his friends and family talk about small-time graft.[22] Want a construction permit? You need to take some cash down to city hall. Get pulled over by a cop? Make sure to hand over a few bills with your driver's license. Dream of starting a new restaurant? Try your cousin's uncle. "You know, petty corruption," MacLean-Abaroa told me.

But MacLean-Abaroa had no idea. On the day that he became mayor, he met with one of the city's accountants, and it turned out that the coffers of La Paz were essentially empty. By the end of the month, there would be no cash, and unless MacLean-Abaroa figured out another solution, he would have to stop paying everyone's salary — including his own — within thirty days. At first, MacLean-Abaroa thought that the problem was the economy. Inflation was running rampant at the time. And yet as he looked closer at the city's budget, he thought something else might be going on, perhaps some corruption or graft.

The extent of the problem didn't really hit MacLean-Abaroa until he arrived at the office for his second day of work, though. The city had given the new mayor a rusted-out 1978 Land Rover with a shattered passenger-side window, and he drove the car home after his first day. The next morning the Land Rover wouldn't start, so MacLean-Abaroa took his own car to city hall. And as he pulled into the city's parking lot, he was surprised to see all sorts of gleaming new cars. How was it possible that La Paz had no money, but some of the civil servants managed to have enough money to buy new cars? MacLean-Abaroa thought.

Then it dawned on him: Everyone was on the take. As MacLean-Abaroa sat in the parking lot, he thought about quitting. He couldn't see a good way out of the situation. How would he wage an anti-corruption war if everyone was corrupt? But MacLean-Abaroa had promised the head of his political party, Hugo Banzer, that he would take the job, and so, like well-meaning politicians around the world, MacLean-Abaroa set out to eradicate corruption. This is a time-honored practice, of course. It seems to happen after every scandal. Someone gets arrested. A stash of money is uncovered. There's a trial. Maybe even a confession. Someone may or may not go to prison.

MacLean-Abaroa didn't really have time to catch people in the act. "I would have had to fire everyone or prosecute everyone," he told me. So instead, he focused on a sort of radical transparency. Almost every aspect of his government would be done out in the open. One of the major sources of corruption, for instance, was the collection of property taxes. MacLean-Abaroa's solution? There would be no more tax assessors, who were easily bribed. Instead, homeowners filled out their own property tax assessments, and the information was published so that people could complain if their neighbor underreported the value of his or her house.

Another huge source of graft was the city's permitting process. When someone wanted to get a license to do construction or open an auto body shop, there were a half dozen ways that city workers could shake them down. So MacLean-Abaroa dramatically simplified the procedure and detailed the rules in a brochure, making it far easier for people to understand the process and file a report if someone asked for a bribe.

When I met MacLean-Abaroa recently, we sat in the back of a small French restaurant a few miles outside of Washington, D.C. He is short and stocky with brown eyes that sparkle with eagerness. He told me how corruption in La Paz dropped significantly during his tenure, and how he eventually became a four-term mayor of the city and a Bolivian presidential candidate. As we spoke, MacLean-Abaroa drew a formula on the paper tablecloth: CORRUPTION = MONOPOLY + DISCRETION − ACCOUNTABILITY.

Tapping the formula with his finger, MacLean-Abaroa explained that when it came to government, managing the power part of the equation — monopoly and discretion — was often the easy part. It was a matter of getting the right level of centralization within the system. The bigger issue was building the type of accountability that didn't devolve into more bribes and payoffs, and for him the answer was transparency because, as MacLean-Abaroa told me, "corruption lives well in the darkness."

When it comes to political trust, openness matters. It encourages oversight, and to hold a government accountable for its actions, people have to know what sort of actions the government is taking. Plus, transparency can engage our social side. When people are honest and forthcoming, we are more likely to trust them. And finally, transparency offers a way to create a type of bottom-up accountability. It empowers citizens. It sustains whistleblowers, and without government transparency, we wouldn't know which schools succeed or which hospitals save lives or how exactly the military spends its budget.

That's not to say that everything should be done out in the open. The pressure for transparency should go upward within a society. Transparency, then, is for the powerful, not the powerless, and within a democracy, it's crucial that people have the ability to vote in secret.[23] Within a company, it's key that people can voice complaints without fear of retribution. This sort of openness, this sort of empowerment, this sort of transparency, can shift the culture of government, and when MacLean-Abaroa returned to La Paz a few years ago, he found that many of his reforms had been rolled back. And yet he felt some satisfaction. Of the four mayors that followed him, three had gone to jail on corruption charges, he said. "Now people know enough to fight back. I destroyed the taboo."

Government can provide a type of floor for our cooperative nature. It can undergird our faith in strangers, and that's crucial to a functioning society, as we saw in the case of Somalia. But there's a problem with this picture, and that's that faith in government doesn't actually begin with good government. Rather, trust in government begins with a sense of society, a shared understanding of goals and values. In a way, we know this already. Or at least we can see it in the data. During times of war, trust in government often goes up, and the September 11 attacks increased faith in Washington by more than twenty percentage points.[24]

The takeaway here is that trust in government requires a sense of commonality, an expectation of prosperity, a feeling of civic pride and ownership. This idea flitted across my mind when I met Paul Zak for the first time. It was a spring afternoon, and as I walked toward him, he opened his arms and embraced me.

"Remember, I'm Dr. Love," Zak told me, referring to one of his nicknames.

On that day, Zak and I sat at a small café not far from the U.S. Capitol building, and I asked him about what he thought the research on oxytocin meant for trust in government. For his part, Zak talked about some of the things that we've already covered. "Transparency is a really key, vital idea for government," he told me. But Zak argues that the recent research on our faith in others suggests a second, just as important strategy. Because if we're wired to connect with others, then we should — as Zak argues — take an approach to rebuilding our sense of society that engages those very connections.

In a way, this is an ancient idea. When the Athenians invented the idea of democracy more than two millennia ago, they built their political system around the notion that everyone should take part in the political process. Thomas Jefferson, too, advocated for active civic involvement. More recently, this idea was central to Robert Putnam's book *Bowling Alone*.

Over the past few years, a number of politicians have taken these ideas to heart and launched innovative initiatives to rebuild a grassroots sense of community. In his writings, Zak discusses the mayor of Bogotá who reduced crime by putting mimes on street corners. I recently spoke to former St. Petersburg mayor Rick Baker, who built dog parks all around the city in order to encourage a greater sense of connection.

But my favorite example remains Bud Clark, who became mayor of Portland in the early 1980s.[25] Clark was nothing like the career politicians who typically won the races for Portland's city hall. He had a woolly beard and a handlebar mustache and owned one of the city's most popular taverns, the Goose Hollow Inn. He called himself a "born-again pagan" and had a distinctive greeting ("*whoop whoop*") and would bike around the city wearing lederhosen.[26] Clark's biggest claim to fame, though, was being the flasher in a poster titled "Expose Yourself to Art."

But Clark won the election in a landslide. The sitting mayor of Portland had run a weak campaign, and the city was struggling. Homelessness was a growing problem. Economic projects had been put on ice, and yet as mayor, Clark didn't just push typical big-city mayor initiatives — better schools, more cops, new jobs. He also dedicated himself to getting people involved, to creating a stronger sense of civic culture.

When it came to reducing crime, Clark thought that the police seemed like an "occupying army," so he encouraged Portland's cops to wear beards and shoulder-length hair to appear more friendly and approachable.[27] Regarding Portland's homeless problem, Clark expanded the city's "sobering station" and encouraged Portlanders to call a special phone number if they ever saw someone passed out.

For Clark it was all about engaging people in the role of government. "I want people to say hi to each other on the street," he once explained.[28] "I think we need to bring an esprit de corps back to Portland." Clark wasn't a pushover. He fired city workers who didn't cut waste. He led a project to build a convention center, and in the end, his citizen-driven approach showed results. Neighborhoods turned around. Unemployment levels dropped. Clark's homeless initiative became a national model.

Still, Clark wanted to be the "people's mayor," and every Thursday he had lunch with whoever came into the office on that day — high school students, city hall reporters, the occasional street person. During the meals, Clark talked about potholes and homework and waivers for obscure city ordinances. He would hear complaints and discuss parades and talk about who might be crowned King Hobo at the annual

Friend of the Hobos festival. "The U.S. is a representative democracy," Clark told me in an email. And that means that "the representatives need to communicate with the citizens that they represent."

There doesn't appear to be any polling data that shows that Clark actually increased trust in government, but consider this: After he left office, a newspaper columnist launched a "Bucks for Bud" initiative to help the former mayor pay down his campaign debts.[29] And even though Clark was no longer running for office, people sent him money. Some of the missives also included pictures. Others held long, appreciative notes. Almost all of the envelopes contained some cash, and the effort eventually pulled in more than thirty thousand dollars.

This doesn't mean that we all should join the local Elks Lodge. Nor do I believe that noontime mayoral lunches are always the answer. But we have to admit that we've lost an important piece of our civic fabric. Looking forward, there are large-scale solutions. Some may lie with the Internet's decentralized ways, and writer Steven Johnson argues that the peer-driven nature of the Internet can work to foster a more dynamic society.[30] In New York, city leaders have created a 311 hotline, which allows people to report everything from missing manhole covers to illegal social clubs. The Obama administration has also pushed a thoughtful "open government" initiative that allows citizens to participate more directly in policy and policymaking.

While many of these efforts to rebuild American government hold promise, so far they've not been enough. When Clark first became mayor of Portland, he was offered a car and driver. But he waved it off and continued to ride his bike into work every day, because it made it easier for voters to approach him with suggestions.[31] Today, of course, it's hard to imagine any big-city mayor refusing a chauffeured car, but the fundamental idea is critical. We need to show trust, to build a culture of community, even if we risk looking like fools. "We all came here [to Oregon] on wagon trains" in search of a better life and new adventures, Clark explained near the end of his time as mayor.[32] "Now we're on the farthest shore we can get to . . . so we've got to make things work."

Chapter 8

Politics

"Encourage You to Be Nasty"

S OME years ago, John Hibbing and Elizabeth Theiss-Morse decided to find out why Americans hated Congress so much, and
the results of their research were both obvious and surprising.[1]
The issue, in short, was democracy itself. Democracy is, of course,
a form of government where everyone has a say — either directly or
through representatives — and by definition, it is filled with conflict
and compromise. The process requires bickering and bargaining. No
one always gets his or her way. Progress is slow. Victories are small.

At least in theory, we're supposed to appreciate all this deliberation.
Robust debate should be a sign that the system is working. But what
Hibbing and Theiss-Morse found was that Americans don't actually
want their politics to be this way. The core aspects of democracy do
not promote the core aspects of trust. When we see politicians debat-
ing each other, we don't view their discussions as signs of a vigorous
democracy.

Instead, for many of us, the back-and-forth between politicians
seems unnecessary. Don't we know the policy solutions already? As
for a compromise, that's even less appealing. When we see a politician
give ground, he or she appears to be pandering. But worst of all, argue
Hibbing and Theiss-Morse, is a careful study of a policy problem. For

most of us, policy solutions seem self-evident, and so a detailed exami-
nation of a proposal seems plainly gratuitous.

Much of the issue is that we don't actually view Congress as an institution that's supposed to be engaged in discourse. Instead, we believe
that Congress is a place for implementation. People "want politicians
to take care of the problems without fuss and without muss, and debates seem completely unnecessary," Theiss-Morse explained to me.
"Americans think politicians are just wasting time and unnecessarily
increasing the conflict level when people believe there is a consensus
and politics should just get the job done."

This distaste for the mechanics of democracy seems to influence
almost every major political event. Look at health care reform as an
example of this idea, as writer Ezra Klein has suggested.[2] When President Obama first proposed reforming the nation's health care system
in February 2009, only around 11 percent of Americans thought the
bill would make their family worse off. But as the debate dragged on,
people began turning against the initiative, and by the time the bill
passed, almost a third of Americans believed that the legislation would
be bad for their families.

The issue didn't seem to be the policy proposals. Even some legisla-
tors might not have known everything that was in the thousand-page
bill. The problem, it seemed, was the raw, unbridled political rancor
that the health care debate inspired. The death panels, the horse trading, the constant backing-and-forthing, it all seemed to undermine the
arguments for the bill's proposals. After all, if the ideas in the bill were
so good, why hadn't anyone implemented them already?

There are some important lessons to take from Hibbing and Theiss-
Morse. Our trust in our political system is a lot like our trust in others.
It's often deeply social. What's more, we often have a far too idealistic
view of democracy, and as political scientist John Mueller points out,
the nature of our political process is such that we never fall into bliss-
ful agreement.[3] Consensus is never reached. Someone always loses.
Winston Churchill once explained that "it has been said that democracy is the worst form of government — except all those other forms
that have been tried." I'd argue that Churchill didn't go far enough.

Democracy is not just the worst form of government. It turns out that if you pay close attention, it can actually be bad for you.

The problem goes deeper than that, though, and our political system has become a case study in how not to build trust. It is rife with two of the traits that might do more than anything to destroy a cooperative culture, extremism and conflicts of interest. In other words, when it comes to social trust and government, there's a deeper problem than issues of bureaucratic oversight or agency transparency. The issue is faith in our nation's political system, and while democracy might be hard and messy, that does not mean it can't be improved. There are better ways to administer a representative form of government — and build the sort of civic community that the nation needs to succeed. To put it simply, the Founding Fathers never expected someone like Newt Gingrich.

Newt Gingrich's political story begins in 1978. Gingrich was a thick, square-headed academic back then. He had run two campaigns for Georgia's Sixth Congressional District, but both efforts had fallen short. Gingrich, it seemed, was the sort of ivory tower academic who just couldn't make it in American politics. But Gingrich decided to run a third campaign, this time against Democrat Virginia Shapard, and he launched a scorched-earth operation that caught many off guard. In TV spots, Gingrich claimed that Shapard supported fraud.[4] "If you like welfare cheaters, you'll love Virginia Shapard," said one commercial. Gingrich also suggested that if Shapard went to Washington, she would be a neglectful mother by leaving her family behind in Georgia. The *Atlanta Journal Constitution* had endorsed Gingrich in his previous two runs for Congress. But the newspaper drew the line in 1978. Gingrich's campaign, the newspaper argued, had devolved into "demagogy and plain lying."[5]

Gingrich won the congressional race against Shapard, and the victory provided a lesson that would frame the rest of his career: When it comes to politics, the ends justify the means. By today's standards, of course, Gingrich's campaign tactics seem almost timid, and over the past three decades, slash-and-burn politics have come to dominate Washington. But Gingrich played a crucial role in developing this sort of bare-knuckle political approach, as Thomas Mann and Norman

Ornstein argue in their excellent book *It's Even Worse Than It Looks,* and the Georgia Republican may have done more than any other single, recent political figure to foster the no-holds-barred political climate that's crippling our nation's democracy.[6]

Gingrich always had big dreams. He once wrote that his primary mission in life was to be a "definer of civilization," and while most members of Congress arrive in Washington wanting to learn the legislative process, Gingrich arrived wanting to get noticed.[7] Even more than your average politician, Gingrich would do whatever it took to land newspaper headlines, and in speeches, he argued that Democratic policies would "murder women and children."[8] Gingrich once explained that one of the Republican Party's "great problems" has been that "we don't encourage you to be nasty."[9]

For Gingrich, these tactics had a clear logic. His political stunts drew attention, and attention, for him, meant a type of power. "The number one fact about the news media," Gingrich once explained, "is they love fights . . . You have to give them confrontations. When you give them confrontations, you get attention; when you get attention, you can educate."[10] At the same time, Gingrich was willing to sacrifice the institutions of democracy in order to achieve his political goals, according to Mann and Ornstein. The House, the Senate, the notion of compromise and cooperation, it didn't seem to matter to Gingrich, if he could achieve his political ends. Or as Republican Trent Lott once told the *New York Times,* "Newt was willing to tear up the system to get the majority."[11]

This sort of twenty-first-century Machiavellianism has its benefits. Gingrich got elected Speaker of the House. He was on the cover of *Time.* The *New York Times* and *Washington Post* wrote long articles about him, and under Gingrich's leadership, the Republicans scored major political victories, including a tax overhaul and welfare reform. But eventually he went too far, and after the failed effort to impeach President Clinton, Gingrich resigned as Speaker in 1998.

Gingrich left behind a new brand of politics, and today many in the GOP have taken up his raw, pit bull style. They're willing, in Mann and Ornstein's words, to engage in the "politics of hostage taking." On this issue, Democrats are just as guilty, and over the years they've engaged in all sorts of winner-takes-all campaigns. For instance, when Senate Majority Leader Harry Reid was asked if Democrats would work with former Republican governor Mitt Romney if he was elected president, Reid made it clear that he would be a pure obstructionist.[12] "Mitt Romney's fantasy that Senate Democrats will work with him to pass his 'severely conservative' agenda is laughable," he explained.

The problem is that our political system isn't meant to have such deeply adversarial parties. Political scientists sometimes call these European- or parliamentary-style political parties.[13] In a parliamentary system, the head of the government — usually called a prime minister — is also the head of the legislative body. In the United States, this would be like the Speaker of the House being president, and in a parliamentary system, the minority party typically works in total opposition to the majority party. But the United States has a presidential system of governance, where the powers of the presidency are separate from the powers of Congress, and within this system, the two opposing parties are generally supposed to work together. But that's not what's happened. Instead, what we have is parliamentary-style political parties in a presidential system, and the result is gridlock.

Extremism has made this problem worse. As a whole, much of the nation is politically middle-of-the-road, and more than a third of Americans identify themselves as moderates in some way.[14] But in recent years, there has been a clear uptick at the edges of both the far left and the far right, and an increasing number of people call themselves very conservative or very liberal. This trend has dramatically shaped the Republican Party, and today the Tea Party faction has significant influence over the GOP's platform. They control who runs in many primaries. They often help decide what issues get attention. This doesn't happen nearly as much on the left, and there's almost nothing on the progressive wing of the Democratic Party that compares to the Tea Party. Only the GOP has an extremist power broker like Senator Ted Cruz.

In many ways, this issue goes farther back than Gingrich. It goes back, in fact, to the creation of the closed primary system, because in a closed primary, only members of the political party can participate, which makes the more extreme elements more powerful.[15] Without nonparty voters, in other words, primary candidates cater more to the political fringe than to the political middle. Even worse has been the deeply partisan drawing of congressional boundaries in recent years. By creating highly gerrymandered districts, political leaders have made moderates an endangered political species, a civic dodo bird, and in many areas there is simply no political fallout for a GOP politician who caters exclusively to the hard-line elements in his or her party.[16]

This change in the GOP has led to odd policy twists. Take Gingrich again, for example. During his early career, the congressman's views weren't particularly extreme. He supported medical marijuana. He believed in climate change. It wasn't clear, Gingrich said, if waterboarding was a type of torture. But when Gingrich ran in the Republican presidential primary in 2012, he veered deeply to the right. Medical marijuana became "a joke."[17] There was no "conclusive proof" of climate change.[18] As for waterboarding? It has become, by Gingrich's analysis, clearly legal.[19] "Waterboarding is, by every technical rule, not torture," he explained.

Politicians should be able to change their minds. That's not the problem. The issue is that extremist, winner-takes-all politics impedes democracy, inhibits good government, and corrodes social trust. And as a nation, we have developed a political system that discourages the very things that civilization depends on: compromise and cooperation.

There have been some experiments with growing moderation. California has a new open-primary system that holds promise. Demographic shifts might help as well, and today's young people are more moderate than their parents. But these are long-term trends. They won't change the fundamentals of the system any time soon. As a congressman, Gingrich once confessed, "I have an enormous personal ambition. I want to shift the entire planet."[20] For Americans, the good news is that the whole planet hasn't shifted. The bad news is that our country has — and we're the worse for it.

Not long ago, neuroscientist Ann Harvey conducted an experiment. The study was fairly straightforward, and Harvey first had subjects evaluate some artwork while they were in an fMRI scanner.[21] The paintings themselves weren't terribly interesting, the sort of stuff that you'd see in a college dorm room — a canvas by Degas, a painting by Picasso. In the scanner, the subjects would rate each artwork on a scale from positive four (love it) to negative four (hate it), and they would be paid $30, $100, or $300 for their time. Harvey added a key wrinkle, though: Before the subjects entered the scanner, they were told that a company had sponsored the experiment and that sometimes the subjects would see the logo of the sponsoring firm next to the work of art.

In many ways, the results of the experiment were what you might expect: If the sponsoring company's logo appeared next to the painting, the subjects were far more likely to say that they enjoyed the artwork. The amount of cash made a difference, too, and the more money that a subject received, the more likely it was that he or she would like the painting. What was surprising, though, was just how unaware the subjects were of their bias. When Harvey asked the subjects if the logo shaped their choices, none of them said that they had been influenced by the company's generosity. And when Harvey looked at the fMRI data, she discovered that the nature of the brain activity made it nearly impossible for someone to even be aware of his or her prejudice. According to Harvey, the bias didn't appear to be something that the subjects could have ever consciously recognized.

What does all this have to do with our nation's political system? A lot, it turns out. Because beyond the general breakdown in political discourse, there's the issue of money, and our political system is flush with cash. We've become so used to this fact that we're immune to the vastness of the problem. But consider for a moment that President Obama raised more than one billion dollars for his 2012 campaign.[22] To put that amount of money into perspective, Facebook bought the online photo-sharing service Instagram for the same amount of money that year. And that's just the start. Mitt Romney wasn't far behind Obama — the GOP presidential candidate also hauled in over a billion dollars. In fact, today many Senate seats cost more than ten million dollars.[23] One recent school board race alone had a three-million-dollar price tag.[24]

Our nation's lawmakers have become beggars in Brooks Brothers clothing. They are constantly searching for cash. They spend huge amounts of time soliciting groups for money. When the Democratic Congressional Campaign Committee recently gave a presentation to new lawmakers, they recommended that new members of Congress spend at least four hours a day dialing up donors.[25] As writer Alex Blumberg recently argued, our nation's lawmakers have two jobs.[26] During the day, they pass — or don't pass — laws. At night, they work as telemarketers. "Most Americans would be shocked — not surprised, shocked — if they knew how much time a U.S. senator spends raising money," Senator Dick Durbin told NPR.

The issue has grown far worse in recent years, and after the Supreme Court knocked down limits on corporate and union money in 2010, outside groups gained the power to fund almost everything. Again, Gingrich's story is illustrative. When the Republican ran for president in 2012, he burned through cash, and for a long time it looked like Gingrich would simply run out of money. But in the closing months of the race, casino magnate Sheldon Adelson wrote a five-million-dollar check to a Super PAC that supported Gingrich — and in a moment, it changed the nature of the campaign.

This is remarkable. A single billionaire was able to keep a presidential candidate afloat — and fundamentally shift the race for the White House. There was nothing illegal about Adelson's donation, of course. In many ways, the gift was average, and in the 2012 election cycle, almost 30 percent of the cash came from some thirty thousand very wealthy individuals.[27] Nor is there much surprising about why Adelson makes such large political donations — the billionaire wants political influence.[28]

Certainly Gingrich would have known that. The former Speaker has long been an expert in the ways that money flows through Washington, and after he left Congress, he built what some called "Newt Inc."[29] Firms paid Gingrich's Center for Health Transformation up to $200,000 for a membership, and in return, the firms got the services of Gingrich. The companies received, according to the firm's marketing documents, "direct Newt interaction."[30]

Our political leaders, it seems, are a lot like the subjects in the fMRI staring at a reproduction of a van Gogh with a little corporate logo in the corner. They think that they're different, that they won't be swayed.

But the evidence suggests that they're wrong. Or take what Adelson once told *Politico*: "I don't believe one person should influence an election," he explained. "So, I suppose you'll ask me, 'How come I'm doing it?' Because other single people influence elections."

Money and politics have long been intertwined, of course. In George Washington's 1758 campaign for the Virginia House of Burgesses, he purchased gallons of rum, brandy, and beer to win over voters at the polling booth.[31] In the early 1850s, Samuel Colt handed out pistols to members of Congress in order to seek support for the passage of a bill.[32] But in recent years, a culture of lobbying has arisen in Washington that's far beyond what the Founding Fathers could have ever imagined. What's remarkable, actually, is the fact that we know it's so bad but we do so little to fight it. Because when we think about what makes people untrustworthy, few things give us more pause than knowing that our partners are in the pocket of someone else. What we need to realize is that every favor does have a price.

When we think about building political trust, there's one final thing to consider, and that's the politicians themselves. Just look at what happened to Al Gore. For a while in September 2000, it seemed likely that Gore would be the next president of the United States, as political scientist Marc Hetherington recounts in his book *Why Trust Matters*.[33] The vice president had beaten expectations at the Democratic Convention. His poll numbers were high. The scandals of the Clinton White House seemed to have faded into memory. In contrast, George W. Bush seemed weak and blunder-prone. The Texas governor's youthful drinking benders were again making headlines, and then, at a campaign event, a hot mike recorded Bush calling a *New York Times* reporter a "major-league asshole."[34]

But then Bush released a political ad that dramatically energized his campaign, according to Hetherington. In a TV spot titled "Trust," Bush speaks directly to the camera.[35] "I believe we need to encourage personal responsibility so people are accountable for their actions," he explains. A few heart-warming scenes then flit across the screen: a mother and her child in the kitchen, some men at a construction site. "That's the difference in philosophy between my opponent and me,"

Bush says. "He trusts government. I trust you." The ad went a long way to define Bush as a politician, as Hetherington argues, and the Texas governor began using the ad's antigovernment message in debates. The Trust ad was played in heavily contested states, and from the moment that the campaign commercial was released until the election, Bush almost never lagged again in the polls.[36]

A decade later, and Bush's approach seems almost stale. "Never trust the government" has become a rallying cry for the Tea Party. "Every day I serve in Congress, I work to fight Washington" was the talking point of one recent Republican messaging document.[37] This isn't an exclusively Republican approach by any means. All sorts of Democrats have run on an anti-Washington message over the years. For politicians, these arguments are an easy way to get ahead. The candidates understand that attacking Washington is an effective way to present themselves as something new. Politicians don't typically bad-mouth the effectiveness of specific federal agencies. They generally don't go after the Marines or the U.S. Postal Service or the Centers for Disease Control. Instead, they present government itself as the problem.

Why does this matter? Well, these political arguments have broader consequences. They stoke fears and anxieties. They foster political cynicism. For Democrats who believe in a more active role for government, the effects have been particularly strong, and research by Hetherington has shown that declining political trust has led to less support for social programs like affirmative action. The lack of trust in government has limited Republicans, too, Hetherington told me in an interview, and without trust in government, many GOP leaders have had a harder time pushing through their agenda.

There's a lot of good news, however. Americans broadly love America, and as I'm sure Thomas Jefferson and John Adams would be happy to know, democracy continues to be highly popular. More than that, the federal government isn't as rife with incompetence as many believe. As political scientist Douglas Amy points out, the government has gone a long way to protect public health, offer consumer protections, and create the strongest military that the world has ever seen. Over the past fifty years, the government has also put a man on the moon, helped map the human genome, and built countless bridges and highways. And despite government shutdowns and debt ceiling crises, we're not heading for a type of Somali dystopia any time soon.

But there's also a real danger. If politicians continue to tell the public not to trust government, then the public won't trust government. Why would they? After all, it's the politicians who are in charge. And in the end, what's surprising, and far worse, is that all of the negative messaging has a terrible impact far beyond Washington: It even influences the nation's murder rate.

It was around four in the morning on October 4, 2009, in Mont Vernon, New Hampshire. Kim Cates and her eleven-year-old daughter, Jaimie, were sleeping together in Kim's bed.[38] Some male voices rang through the dark house.

"Jaimie, is that you?" Kim Cates called out.[39]

Two men were standing at the side of the bed. They had a machete and a long knife, and they began hacking at Cates and her daughter.

"Please don't do it," Kim Cates called out. "No. Please, no."

The men waited until the bodies appeared lifeless. Then they roamed the house, taking whatever appeared valuable. Some jewelry boxes. A pearl necklace. All in all, it wasn't much. But the men didn't care. That's not why they were there. One of the young men, Christopher Gribble, later bragged that the murder had been "awesome."[40] The second man, Steven Spader, told the same friend that he wanted to "do it" again.[41] Neither of the two killers knew Cates. They had broken into her house because it was secluded, and the two promised each other to kill whoever they found inside. Within days, police arrested Gribble and Spader, and after a trial, the two men received life sentences without parole.

Historian Randolph Roth begins his book *American Homicide* with a different murder, and he comes to a simple conclusion that extends to almost every homicide: The court-approved, appears-in-the-newspaper account doesn't explain all that much about why people actually murder each other. Motives, Roth argues, "say very little about what shapes the mindset of murderers . . . to become killers." More than that, the court-approved, appears-in-the-newspaper account doesn't explain why murder rates differ across cultures, as Roth points out.

There must be something in our history, then, that explains why Americans kill each other so much. After all, we have three times the murder rate of Canada, and ten times the rate of some of the world's least murderous nations.[42] No other first-world democracy has higher homicide levels than the United States, according to Roth, and today, almost one out of every two hundred American children will die at the hands of someone else.

Some two decades ago, Roth began looking more closely into why exactly our nation's murder rates are so high. At the time, most experts believed that the cause was a mix of social and economic issues. Unemployment, weak salaries, crack cocaine — these were supposed to be the engines of homicide. But when Roth analyzed historical databases, he uncovered a different set of causes. It turned out that the less people felt connected to others, the more likely they were to murder each other, and when our political leaders seem incompetent or divisive, people become aggrieved. They feel disconnected, and so they're more likely to kill.

Other criminologists have come to similar conclusions as Roth, but on a smaller scale. In the 1990s, for instance, sociologist Gary LaFree showed that over the previous fifty years, attitudes toward government closely tracked homicide rates. Roth takes a longer view, going all the way back to the seventeenth century, and it turns out that King Philip's War led to a sudden drop in the murder rate by creating a sense of solidarity among the early colonists. And the biggest jump in the nation's murder rates? That occurred after Watergate. As the nation became disenchanted with politicians — and society itself — an increasing number of people killed each other.

But perhaps what's most surprising might be the power of feeling connected to others. "People's views about the legitimacy of government and about their fellow citizens correlate so strongly with how often they kill unrelated adults — much more strongly than other factors such as guns, poverty, drugs, race, or a permissive justice system," Roth explained to me.

Take, for instance, the two men who murdered Kim Cates. Christopher Gribble had grown up isolated. His parents had homeschooled him. As a teenager, he would wear the same camouflage outfit day after day, and during the trial, he showed little remorse. "I thought I would feel bad," Gribble explained.[43] "I'm almost sorry to say I don't. I thought I would at least puke afterward or something." The other killer, Steven Spader, was an only child who had dropped out of high school. After the homicide, he wrote a letter to the Nashua *Telegraph* arguing that he and his friends were different. Outsiders simply didn't understand them. He dismissed the public as "brainless conformists."[44]

To be clear, the solution isn't for politicians to tell people to stop killing others, though certainly that can help. Instead, thoughtful leaders promote a sense of togetherness, an overall feeling of community, and homicide levels dropped under inclusive presidents such as Eisenhower and Clinton, according to Roth. In other words, when it comes to governing, a little trust can go a long way.

Chapter 9

Technology

Communication, Community, and Couchsurfing

C ASEY Fenton was going to Iceland. He wanted a local, Reykja-
vikian sort of travel adventure while he was there, so he began
hunting through the University of Iceland student directory,
pulling out every email that he could find.[1] Fenton fired off more than
a thousand messages. "Hi, I'm coming to Iceland next week," the emails
read. "It would be nice to hang out. What can we do?"

Fenton ultimately got back between fifty to a hundred responses,
and he decided to hang out with an Icelandic woman named Johanna.
"She had been on the cover of an Icelandic tabloid, and I thought: Fascinating. When else am I going to hang out with a controversial Icelandic socialite?" Fenton told me. Johanna gave Fenton an insider's tour
of Iceland. They went drinking with Johanna's friends. Fenton visited
Johanna's family, who lived near the ocean, and when he left the country a few days later, he thought to himself: *This is how I'll have to travel
all the time.*

After Fenton returned home, he realized that others wanted to have
similar travel adventures, and a few years later, he started a website
called Couchsurfing. The idea behind the site was straightforward —
locals who have an empty bed or couch offer it to visitors who are
looking for a place to stay. When the site first went up, the typical user
was what you might imagine: a twenty-five-year-old trekking through

Bangkok, hunting for a place to stash his backpack and drink red wine in a coffee mug.

But over the past few years, the site has dramatically expanded its audience, and today it might be one of the world's most successful travel networks. There are more than six million members, some twenty million dollars in venture capital funding, and listings on the site include everything from a Bedouin cave in Jordan to an oceanside apartment in Portugal. "We're trying to build the feeling that the world is larger than you think, that it's safer than you think, that it cares about more than you think," Fenton told me.

I first came across Fenton and the connection between trust and Couchsurfing in the excellent book *What's Mine Is Yours* by Rachel Botsman and Roo Rogers. In their book, Botsman and Rogers detail the rise of what they call "collaborative consumption," and they argue that sites like Couchsurfing can work "to bind us together." For Botsman and Rogers, collaborative consumption sites like Airbnb, Zipcar, and Freecycle build an important type of social capital because they help connect people who might not otherwise be bonded. (Yochai Benkler also discusses Couchsurfing in his work. But it was the *New Yorker* that might have had the most entertaining discussion of the website. The headline of the *New Yorker* article? "You're Welcome.")

I wanted to know more about Couchsurfing and how it might improve our faith in others, and so when I traveled to Roanoke, Virginia, recently, I used the site to connect with Andres Moctezuma. He lived just outside of downtown Roanoke in a sprawling house with a hot tub, five bedrooms, and an exercise room complete with free weights and motivational posters. On the site, Moctezuma described himself as a "half-Mexican half-Polish guy with extraordinary good luck." His personality, he added, was a bit like a dog's, "the ones that run free and don't come when they are called." When I told my wife about my plans, she gave me a quizzical look that said: *Really?*

But my evening with Moctezuma in Roanoke had the genial feeling of meeting a distant cousin for the first time. He took me for drinks at a local Cuban restaurant. We talked about how Moctezuma once surfed the waves in Puerto Escondido, Mexico. He told me about the time that he practiced aikido in a dojo in Tokyo. Moctezuma has used

Couchsurfing dozens of times, staying at other people's houses as well as hosting. His worst experience? The time that a mother and daughter stayed at his house, and while he was at work, the women reorganized all of his dishes. "They were trying to be nice, but it was a little weird," he told me. "I remember not being able to find my bowls for a while."

If that's a bad experience, it's not all that bad, and most surfers have positive interactions. Crime is relatively rare, and as many as 18 percent of surfers reciprocate an exchange, which suggests that the interaction went well enough for people to want to see each other again.[2] In other words, people are living up to Fenton's expectation that the world is much safer than you think, that it cares about you much more than you think.

That certainly was the experience of Edward Chu. He had used Couchsurfing a few times before he arrived in New York City's Penn Station a few years ago. The bus ride from Lexington, Virginia, had taken Chu nine hours, and when he stepped onto the streets of Manhattan, it was like entering an arcade game. Everything seemed bright and shimmery. At the time, Chu was in his second year at the Virginia Military Institute. The school was a good fit for him. He loved the deep traditions (first-year students at the school are called "rats") and the self-discipline (telephone use on campus is limited).

Chu was on Thanksgiving break, and during his trip to New York City, he planned to stay a few nights at the apartment of Bob Redmond.[3] Chu had met Redmond through Couchsurfing, and typically users will check the profile of the host before they visit to gain a sense of the person's reputation. But Chu had been in a rush that morning, and he never got a chance to glance at Redmond's profile.

Finally, sometime around midnight, Chu arrived at the building, rode the elevator to the sixth floor, and then knocked on Redmond's door. A moment passed and the door was pulled open, and today Chu can't quite remember what happened next. Did he step inside? Did he drop his bags? The one thing that Chu can remember is that Redmond was naked.

Chu recalls feeling a sort of shock. His face blanched. He put his arm over his eyes. "Oh no," he said. "Oh no."

"You didn't check my profile, did you?" Redmond asked.

The two men stood awkwardly in the hallway while Redmond explained that he was a nudist, that he had not worn clothes at home for decades.

"I felt a little better after I met his roommates," all of whom wore clothes, Chu told me later. "But yeah, it was pretty weird." Yet for all the weirdness, Chu stayed at Redmond's apartment for a few nights. During the day, Chu would visit tourist sites. At night, he would have dinner with Redmond and some of Redmond's friends. One night, filet mignon; another night, turkey. It turned out that they both loved Broadway shows and traveling. Redmond asked Chu about what it was like to attend a military school, while Chu became comfortable with Redmond's nudism. "I would find it weird if Bob had clothes on now," Chu told me.

The two men became friends of a sort, and when Chu came to New York City two years later, he again stayed at Redmond's apartment. One Saturday morning during that second visit, I joined them for brunch. Redmond was, of course, naked. It was easy to spot his favorite chair, too: He kept a towel over the top of the seat to keep it clean. We talked about Couchsurfing and military academies and what it was like to answer the door naked.

The two men were, without question, an odd pair. One was a middle-aged gay nudist; the other, a twentysomething military student. But they laughed and joked and talked about an off-Broadway show that they had seen together. They weren't the closest of buddies. But they had developed a type of bond. Or as Chu told me, "I didn't think this would happen, but I'd say that Bob is one of my friends."

It might be hard to believe that technology can promote trust. An iPad is supposed to foster isolation. People believe that Facebook makes us lonely. But it turns out that technology can kick-start our cooperative ways. One way to understand this idea is to start with some phone calls that came into the BMW service desk some years ago. The German car company had put in a new GPS system that spoke to drivers in a female voice, and a short time later, men started calling the car company and complaining. Clifford Nass served as a consultant to BMW at the time, and in his book *The Man Who Lied to His Laptop*, he recounts a typical exchange between the drivers and the BMW customer service operators:

> Customer: I can't use my navigation system.
> Operator: I'm very sorry about that, sir. What seems to be the problem?
> Customer: A woman should not be giving directions.
> Operator: Sir, it is not really a woman. It is only a recorded voice.
> Customer: I don't trust directions from a woman.
> Operator: Sir, if it makes you feel better, I am certain that the engineers that built the system and the cartographers who figured out the directions were all men.
> Customer: It doesn't matter. It simply doesn't work.[4]

Because of the spate of calls, BMW ultimately recalled the device, and the reason was obvious: The male drivers didn't like women telling them what to do. This incident goes beyond the narrow-mindedness of well-heeled drivers, and the anecdote underscores the fact that our brains interact with technology in much the same way that they interact with individuals. Our brains often view devices as social beings, and if you are the type of man who doesn't think that a woman should be giving you directions, then you don't want a woman's voice giving you directions.

Why does this happen? Well, we're social machines, and our brains weren't built to distinguish between a person and a piece of technology that acts like a person. "For almost all of human history, if something acted like a human, sounded like a human, it was a human," Nass told me. "Our brains did not evolve for anything else."

In one study, Nass asked users to give feedback on a software package.[5] The first group used the software package on one computer and then answered questions about its performance on the same computer. The second group used the same software but responded to questions on a different computer. It turned out that the people who both tested and reviewed the software on the same computer gave the software better ratings. The explanation is simple, according to Nass. The subjects tried to protect the computer's feelings; they didn't want to tell the device that it had presented them with bad software.

Part of the issue is that the physical world and our mental representations of it are deeply connected, and within our brains, fiction isn't all that fictional. Imagination isn't all that imaginative. When I called Nass for an interview, he was in Palo Alto, California, and he pointed out that my brain had probably created a mental image of him, making it seem like we were talking face-to-face even though he was some three thousand miles away.

Paul Zak has also done informal experiments that help us better understand this idea, and it turns out that when people log in to a social network and interact with close friends, their oxytocin increases. Zak conducted the first of these studies with journalist Adam Penenberg, and in his accompanying *Fast Company* article, Penenberg argues that the results suggest that "online relationships can be just as real as those conducted offline."[6]

This notion fascinated me, and when I visited Zak at his home, I asked the neuroscientist to give me the same experiment that he had given Penenberg. So Zak took my blood. I spent some ten minutes on Facebook. And then Zak took my blood again. The results were the same as Penenberg's: After I messaged friends and posted pictures of my daughter, my trust hormone jumped up. It was, as Zak argues, like the virtual world wasn't really all that virtual, as if the picture of my daughter wasn't all that different than seeing her in person.

I'd argue that one of the reasons that we have such a negative view of technology goes back to the television. In *Bowling Alone,* for instance, Robert Putnam suggests that TV has gone a long way to corrupt our sense of togetherness. He points out that television watchers are less engaged, less friendly, even less happy, and Putnam argues that as much as 15 percent of civic apathy lies at the feet of what he calls the TV generation. Putnam might be right. But what's crucial — and perhaps too obvious to point out — is that the Internet is fundamentally different from television. Or look at something like Couchsurfing: There's simply no way that your old Panasonic could have created that type of experience. It wouldn't have made the personal connection. It couldn't have supported the level of communication.

Of course, what makes the Internet different — and more power-ful — does not always make us more trusting, and certainly some of our technology usage can make us more isolated. Part of the issue is that a lot of the screen time is plainly mindless. When I recently ana-lyzed a federal database, I found that kids in school generally don't use digital devices for high-end interactive programs like simulations.[7] Instead, they're honing basic skills, and more than a third of middle school math students regularly use a computer for drill and practice. In contrast, only 24 percent of middle school students regularly use spreadsheets for math assignments. In high schools, I uncovered a similar trend, and an overwhelming proportion of students reported regularly watching a movie or video in science class, while well under half said they've had "hands-on experience with simple machines."

The Internet doesn't always make us more honest either, and the Web allows people to be anonymous, hidden. Or as the classic *New Yorker* cartoon notes: "On the Internet, no one knows you're a dog." Sometimes this promotes transparency. But just as often it makes it harder to figure out if your partner is trustworthy. For their part, smart tech companies understand the limitations of technology, and they take steps to encourage face-to-face interaction, with some, like the peer-to-peer lending firm Zilok, requiring people to meet in person before they exchange services. "This is actually quite important," Zilok cofounder Gary Cige told me. "Because you are actually less likely to screw someone that you've already met and will meet again."

The bottom line is that the principles of trust don't change when it comes to technology. Reciprocity will always be a way to build our faith in others. Connectedness will always matter, and when we use technology in thoughtful ways, it can sometimes be easier for these principles to take hold.

When technology works for us, it does more than build new oppor-tunities for communication. It can also build vast networks and infor-mation systems. It can create communities and social movements. It can even personalize something as impersonal as your microwave. But there's a problem with technology, as security expert Bruce Schneier argues: Technology helps both the world's saints and its sinners.

Take, for instance, the story of Robert Morris. On November 2, 1988, he was sitting in front of a computer at Cornell University. He was a first-year computer science grad student with shaggy hair and Andy Warhol–style glasses.[8] For the previous few weeks, Morris had been tinkering with a program designed to reveal some of the security holes in an early computer network called Arpanet. The Department of Defense had built Arpanet as a way to connect computers to each other, and the network eventually evolved into what we know today as the Internet. Back then, though, Arpanet was still fairly new, linking around sixty thousand computers in research facilities and military bases around the country.

Robert Morris knew computers well, as Katie Hafner and John Markoff describe in their book *Cyberpunk*. As an undergrad, Morris had become a bit of a computer science legend at Harvard, and even before graduate school, he had given speeches on computer safety at the National Security Agency. Soon after Morris arrived at Cornell, he became curious about just how large and interconnected Arpanet had become. So over the course of a few weeks, Morris created a few lines of code that would burrow through the network. "My purpose was to write a program that would spread as widely as possible," he later explained.[9] Morris released his computer program into the Arpanet system at around 7:30 on that November evening, and when he came back after dinner, he couldn't get into his computer. The machine was down. Morris soon figured out what had gone wrong: His code was replicating far faster than he had thought possible. When Morris built the program, he assumed that it would move across the network slowly. But the code was rushing through Arpanet, clogging the network, flooding computers, and crashing systems. "I was scared; it seemed like the worm was going out of control," he later explained.[10]

Morris managed to have an anonymous message sent out that night, detailing how network managers could potentially stop the program. But it was too late. The network had already been pushed over its limit, and around 10 percent of all Arpanet-linked computers became infected. In some places, Morris's computer program destroyed entire networks, and the Army Ballistics Research Laboratory in Aberdeen,

Maryland, had to shutter its laboratories for almost a week. "It was like the *Sorcerer's Apprentice*," one researcher later explained.[11]

Morris had unleashed the world's first computer worm. A computer worm is different from a computer virus. A virus needs a program or application to function, and viruses usually require someone to do something in order to infect a computer. But a worm can travel across computers without anyone's help, and a worm's ability to propagate itself across a network underscores a paradox that's at the heart of technology: The more connected we are, the more vulnerable we are. Take Arpanet again. The network of computers blazed the way for Skype and Tumblr and Etsy. But it also made each device within the system more vulnerable to attack, and so a mild-mannered grad student was able to bring down the research arm of an army base.

This all works to make security a never-ending sort of struggle, as Schneier and many others have argued. It's an endless competition. I recently spoke to security expert Brian Chess. He serves as the vice president of security and infrastructure at a technology firm, and he's constantly uncovering new attacks on the company's software. Hackers will invent a new virus or expose a new operating system loophole, and Chess will have to create a program that stops the attack.

But the hackers will soon come up with a more sophisticated invasion, and so Chess has to develop a more sophisticated defense. This continues, he told me, more or less every day. "We put a defensive system in place. The bad guys look at that and then they come back at that," he told me. "We just walk up the ladder together."

Schneier argues that societies reach a sort of equilibrium between what he calls the doves (the people who protect security systems) and the hawks (the people who break into security systems). The problem is that technology disrupts the balance — and often gives an initial advantage to the hawks. "The marginal, the unorganized, they incorporate new technology a lot faster than the institutional," Schneier told me.

The doves face other problems, as Schneier points out, and too much security can crowd out our social side. It can make us less trusting. Plus, security tends to push out nuance. Take the Robert Morris case again. A jury eventually found the graduate student guilty of hacking, and a judge sentenced him to three years of probation and a $10,000 fine, which is nearly the same punishment a man received a few years later for sexually abusing a ten-year-old.[12]

Schneier has long argued that "security is a process," and he's absolutely right. We're always walking up the security ladder together, as Brian Chess told me, and technology highlights this balancing act. What's striking, I think, is that social trust isn't all that different. It's also a process, something that develops over time, something that we grow and create, a manifestation of our social capital. What Schneier suggests is that technology just underscores the notion that trust of any sort can't be guaranteed. We can take solace in the fact that when we trust, we're typically rewarded with more trust. We can take solace in the fact that people are generally trustworthy. But trust is also risk, and without that risk, cooperation wouldn't be cooperation. It would be subservience.

Chapter 10

Path Forward

Sometimes We Need to Leap

HEIGHTS have put me in a panic for as long as I can remember. I hate balcony seating. I don't like looking at tall buildings. A ride on an escalator can send me into a roar of shivers. I'm not against a little thrill-seeking. I've owned motorcycles. I've raced cars. My problem is high places, and the Greek myth of Icarus never made much sense to me. I've never seen it as much of a cautionary tale. It's more like a story of the obvious. Forget about the sun melting the wax of his wings. Who cares about his hubris. Of course, Icarus should have spiraled to his death. He tried to soar in the sky. What else could he expect?

But still, near the end of my research for this project, I decided to go skydiving. I had spent more than a year researching issues of social trust, and I wanted to see what I had learned. Are we really that trusting — and trustworthy? Is there a scientific basis for our cooperative ways? Is there a way to rebuild our social fabric? I was also inspired by writers like Jeff Wise, who went skydiving for science for his engaging book *Extreme Fear*.[1]

We know that fight-or-flight chemicals shoot up when people are scared, of course. But what would happen to oxytocin? Would intense fear also cause the trust hormone to shoot up? It shouldn't. Fear is an ego-driven emotion, and when the stress hormone cortisol rockets through our bodies at full blast, the limbic system takes over. Pain feels distant. Muscles tighten. Blood vessels expand. Thoughts become narrow and focused, and when psychologists give cognitive tests before high-stress events, people are often unable to answer a basic question like what's three plus nine. To put it differently, fight-or-flight isn't just a response system. It can become an autopilot system that takes over our bodies.

Zak knew this as well as anyone, and in studies, he's found that when people have high levels of cortisol, they tend to act more selfishly. In economic games, they're not as trusting or as trustworthy.[2] During stressful events, testosterone levels also often spike, and the male hormone has a different effect than cortisol. Testosterone builds strong muscles and thick beards. It encourages risk taking and makes people less trustworthy. Basically, it's what makes people act like they're aggressive, entitled teenagers. In another experiment, Zak asked subjects to write down what they believed an "acceptable" offer would be from a partner in an economic game, and with a shot of testosterone, the subjects would reject their own offer around 10 percent of the time. With a placebo, it was just 3 percent.

Still, Zak believes that our oxytocin-based bonding system remains strong even in the most heart-thumping moments, so when a graduate student mentioned skydiving as a way to test his theory, Zak thought: *Great idea.* Zak had already done two experiments on himself, and each time, he sampled his blood before and after he went skydiving. The results were hardly scientific. These were illustrative examples.

But the data were suggestive. Zak's cortisol levels skyrocketed, and on the first dive, the stress hormone jumped 400 percent. More surprisingly, Zak's oxytocin levels also ticked upward, increasing more than 40 percent. "It's remarkable that the oxytocin system works in this sort of situation," Zak told me. "I mean, think about it. You're literally scared for your life."

In the weeks before the jump, I thought a lot about Zak's "scared for your life" comment. Way too much, actually. Low-level panic attacks would strike without warning. In the middle of the afternoon, sitting in my office, I'd imagine myself jumping out of the airplane, and my chest would grow empty. My hands would tremble. I'd start to cough and choke. Over time, I became convinced that when it came to oxytocin, Zak must have been an outlier. Why would your body release a social hormone if you were convinced that you were about to die?

My fears grew worse, and the night before the jump, I had friends witness the signing of my will. I took a horse-sized dose of Ambien but still couldn't sleep. My body was nervous and twitchy, and by the time I arrived at the skydiving center the next day and met up with Zak, it felt like panic had short-circuited my brain. I couldn't seem to make any sort of decision. Would I need sunglasses? Should I bring a snack? Did I need to go to the bathroom one more time? My brain couldn't quite get a fix on the answers.

Then, much sooner — and much later — than I had hoped, Zak had drawn my blood, and I was shaking hands with my skydiving instructor, Christiaan Rendle. He was broad-shouldered and ponytailed, and I pestered him with one query after another. *How often have you been skydiving? Ever had any problems? Did you pack our parachute?* It turned out that Rendle was one of the most experienced instructors at the skydiving center. He had done some fourteen thousand jumps and had served as a stunt double in movies and TV commercials. As for the parachute, he didn't pack it himself, and yes, there was a second parachute in case the first one didn't work.

Rendle hustled me into the plane along with Zak and his skydiving instructor, and what happened next is a jumbled sequence of vivid snapshots. The hawkish profile of the pilot's face. Another skydiving instructor telling some corny jokes. Rendle snapping me into what was essentially an adult-sized baby carrier.

In the plane, Zak sat a few feet away from me. "You all right, Ulrich?"

A dull pain roiled my stomach. Sweat coated my palms. Someone had already jumped from the plane, but the thundering noise made it too loud to hear any of his screams. It seemed like the sky had just swallowed him alive.

"Yup, I'm good!" I yelled back.

Then, endless minutes later, Zak and his skydiving instructor bellyflopped out of the plane. And then, slowly, like some sort of barely working stop-motion movie, step by slow step, foot by slow foot, Rendle and I hobbled to the open door. I was swaddled by then, and Rendle more or less had to shove me out into the sky.

"Holy fucking shit! Holy fucking shit!" I kept screaming at 120 miles per hour, my body stretched out like a kite. In midair, as I was plunging downward in a screaming, explosive rush, Rendle tapped me, reminding me to release my grip on my harness, and then without warning, after a long velocity-filled high, it was over, and the parachute opened up above us like a giant nylon cloud.

As we floated to the ground, I quickly re-realized my fear of heights, my deep hatred of being off the ground, and eventually I landed on a grassy field. Zak quickly escorted me back to skydiving center, where he would take my blood. I knew, of course, that I had trusted Rendle that afternoon. But would my oxytocin levels go up? I wasn't sure, or as Zak told me, "You looked like a robot up there."

Zak turned out to be half right, and before the jump, my oxytocin was at bottom-of-the-test-tube levels. It seemed as if there was barely a peptide of the trust hormone floating around in my blood. But after the leap, my oxytocin levels had leapt upward by 193 percent. "Huge trust response," Zak explained. I looked at the results for my other hormones. They had increased, but not nearly as much as oxytocin. My testosterone levels were up 8 percent. Cortisol levels increased 9 percent.

At first I thought that I must have experienced some sort of special oxytocin high. Why else would my oxytocin levels have increased so much? But Zak explained that my cortisol levels would have gone up higher if they hadn't been so sky-high to start off with. "Your ACTH baseline was through the roof," he explained. "Same with your testosterone. You were so pumped up for the jump that there was little your body could do to get you more amped up during the free fall."

Given what we know about stress, it's obvious why my cortisol and testosterone levels increased. But it's not at all clear what might have prompted oxytocin release. When I reached out to neuroscientist Larry Young, he told me that the cause may have been dopamine. "Perhaps the excitement of skydiving stimulated oxytocin release, which then could make the social cues of whoever you are with more salient,"

Young wrote in an email. "Perhaps when a couple of guys fight off and kill a lion, they feel the exhilaration but also develop a bond."

I also contacted Sue Carter, who had done the groundbreaking research on prairie voles, and she argued that oxytocin can provide a type of emotional buffer for stress. "Oxytocin helps with coping," Carter explained. The final thing to consider is something far simpler. My oxytocin levels were so low before the jump that the hormone probably had only one way to go: upward.

Zak is not sure what the results mean either. There were too many variables. This wasn't a science experiment; it was an anecdote. Zak's current theory — and it's very much a theory — is that even in these extreme I'm-going-to-die moments, we want to connect with others. We want to develop a bond. It's not that we want others to help us, though clearly that's part of it. Rather, our attachment circuits are creating a meaningful partnership. They're developing a learned sense of: *This person saved my life, and so I want to be around him. I want to help him. And when I return the favor, it will feel good.* "My guess is that the first thing in your mind when the parachute pulled open was: 'I love this guy so much,'" Zak told me.

As evidence, Zak pointed to the fact that people often have very clear memories of their skydiving instructors, and certainly I could easily recall Rendle's narrow eyes, brown ponytail, and easy demeanor. "If you see your skydiving instructor on the street five years from now, I guarantee you that you'll recognize him. His face will be imprinted on your brain. You've bonded with him. You see him as a friend," Zak told me. "As far as your mind goes, he saved your life. But I don't think he'll remember you. I mean, he does jumps with dozens of different people every day."

The data suggest that the brain's bonding system works even in the most stressful of stressful situations, although that still needs to be confirmed. "A two hundred percent increase in oxytocin is extraordinarily rare in all the experiments we've run, and you had it under such high levels of stress and testosterone," Zak told me. "It really tells you that we have a powerful kind of survival system around connection and oxytocin, and if we want to understand human nature, human society, this is a big part of the story."

For Zak, the point is that even when we're supposed to be at our most selfish, even when our lives are on the line, we're built to connect. For centuries we've referred to our species as *Homo sapiens,* which comes from the Latin for "wise man," but I think we've been wrong. Our cooperative ways, our social side, has often mattered far more for the success of our species than our "wisdom," and we might be better off thinking of ourselves as *Homo confido,* or "trusting man." That, it seems, is a more accurate description of who we are.

Daredevil Felix Baumgartner once argued that when people go skydiving, they get a sense of the immensity of the world.[3] But Baumgartner got it only half right. Because when you jump out of a plane attached to someone else, you also learn about the immensity of our faith in others, and it turns out that skydiving serves as a metaphor for how we might create a more trusting — and trustworthy — society.

The first lesson? We need to do more to consider the perspectives of others. When I first met my skydiving instructor, Christiaan Rendle, he told me that he had a sense of what I was going through. He didn't joke about it. He didn't make me feel spineless or simpleminded. "For a lot of people this is probably one of the most adventurous things they'll ever do," Rendle told me. "They might spend six months planning it, thinking about it, building it up. I always try and remind myself that this is a big deal for people." In other words, even after having done more than fourteen thousand jumps, Rendle tries to show some sympathy for first-timers.

When it comes to trust, building faith in friends and family is often relatively easy. What's harder — and, frankly, far more important — is building faith in people outside of your group. Almost every expert in social ties — from Paul Zak to Robert Putnam to Frans de Waal — highlights the importance of this issue, and indeed, it's at the very center of social trust. Or better yet, ask yourself: Do I interact with people who look different from me? Do I engage with people who have diverse political views? Do I spend time with people who make more or less money than I do?

In this sense, journalist Robert Wright had it right when he recently argued that one of the nation's most pressing issues was the fact that people don't look at problems "from the point of view of other people."[4] As Wright suggests, this means that if you're a gun owner, you might need to understand that not everyone shares your passion for assault rifles. And if you're not a gun owner, it means realizing that people who buy guns often see their weapons as a civil right.

The second lesson is that trust is ultimately a choice. Before I jumped out of the plane at Skydive Elsinore, I had to take a short class and watch a training video. The instructor reviewed all the key lessons with me as well. I knew exactly what I was getting into. This helps explain why schooling often leads to higher levels of social trust; with more education, we're more understanding. This idea also goes back to the story of subway driver Hector Ramirez. We want people to have their own sense of right and wrong. We want people to have a feeling of autonomy. As a society, we don't want to force trust. We want to grow trust.

The third lesson is one that football coach Bill Walsh might have expressed best: "Success belongs to everyone." Or consider this anecdote: Shortly before Rendle and I stepped into the plane, I joked that it should be easy for me to trust him. After all, if Rendle made a mistake, we would both plummet to our deaths. But Rendle quickly corrected me, pointing out that we needed to work together. If I didn't arch my back, the two of us could flip over in midair and potentially have a dangerous landing. He made it clear that we were in the jump together, that we needed to work as partners.

And finally there's this fact: No one wants to jump out of a plane with a hole in his parachute, and when we think about trust, we also need to think about trustworthiness. At the micro level, we need to focus on ourselves. If we want the faith of others, we need to ask: Am I honest? Am I dependable? Do I deliver results? For individuals, the trust-building process doesn't so much begin with faith. It begins with reliability and performance, and we often overestimate how much others believe that we are trustworthy.[5]

At the macro level, the questions around trustworthiness are similar. Do our institutions inspire trust by being productive, transparent, and accountable? Does our society promote justice and equality? Does our economy ensure that everyone gains? There's no doubt that many of our institutions could do better. Within government, agencies will sometimes fail to track performance and show that they are, in fact, responsible and outcome-oriented. Our justice system doesn't do nearly enough to build a sense of shared values either, and too often individuals view our legal system as unfair — and illegitimate.

Or just consider our nation's ever-growing levels of inequality. Because of the yawning gap between the rich and poor, we're less likely to trust — and less optimistic about our future.[6] In a way, we're coming across an idea that we've already seen: When it comes to our faith in others, trustworthiness is the difference between trusting well and trusting poorly. And we need to do more to build this sort of trustworthiness — and this sort of trust. That means stronger communities. That means a deeper social fabric. That means understanding that trust is ultimately a risk — one that might not always pay off. But above all, it's time to leap.

Acknowledgments

While I worked on this project, I often wondered why anyone would write a book on trust. Could I have chosen a broader, more ill-defined subject? Maybe a book on love? War? The history of civilization? More to the point, there were lots of times when I doubted myself, when I relied on others to get me through. Above all, then, an unending thank-you to my wife, Nora. Without your love and support, I'd still be rewriting the first page. My daughters, Leila and Sonja, made me realize that trust is a type of love, and my faith in you will always endure. Since I was a kid, my parents have never stopped encouraging me. Dad, your creativity still inspires. Mom, I'm *still* waiting for cookbook number two. My brother and sister were a wonderful help, too. Markus, to quote your feedback: "Tumescent twinge = hard-on? Why tell at all?" And, Katharina, who knew that Simon Baron-Cohen was so hard to reach? Oh, Rachel and Bryan: The circle of trust extends to you, too. Next time I'll be filling up your inbox with a draft manuscript.

My profound gratitude goes to Carly Hoffmann. Your attention to detail, your enduring support, thank you; and, no, I don't know why the Alaskans are so trusting. Gillian McKenzie is a literary agent with vision and grit. She contributed hugely to this book, or as she wrote once in an email, "*The Leap* is catchy!" To David Moldawer: Thanks for seeing the promise in a rough idea. I hope we get to work together on a project soon. To Katie Salisbury: Your advice has been spot-on, down to the recommendation about me smiling in my author photo.

Thank you for pushing this project over the finish line. And to my copyeditor, Douglas Johnson, an endless thank you.

At the Center for American Progress, I had a deeply supportive group of colleagues, including Kristina Costa, Gadi Dechter, John Podesta, Reece Rushing, and Neera Tanden. Without the inspiration of the Doing What Works project, I would have never embarked on this project. A special thanks to Cindy Brown, who gave me the time off to work on this book. Oh, and I hope you don't find a typo. And then there's the brilliant Carl Chancellor, whose wonderful editorial help got me over the finish line.

To my first readers, thank you again for the careful read, and my deepest gratitude goes to Josh Christianson, Justin Ewers, Wray Herbert, Caitlin Kelley, David Madland, and Rich Shea. I couldn't have completed this project without the support of an excellent team of research assistants, transcribers, and stringers, including Jeric Aspillaga, Muhire Enock, Nicholas Forster, Max McClure, Gary Sarli, Chelsea Shover, and Emma Zaballos. A shout-out to Derek Shaffer for the continued nonlegal legal advice. This time, I'll get your name spelled right.

I owe a significant debt to Austin Frerick. Is there an obscure academic study that you can't find? Thank you to Eva Dasher for her excellent research skills. She triple-checked some facts, including the spelling of her own name. There's a long list of people who were interviewed but never made it into the pages of the book, and I also wanted to thank Elissar Andari, Rick Baker, John Bradshaw, Seth Goldman, Donald Green, Rich Hephner, Marc Hoogsteyns, Bert Ingelaere, Margaret Levi, Daniel Olguin, Denis Regan, Jacob Resneck, Lisa Hare Ridgley, Erin Kaplan Rupolo, Michelle Self, Jason Shaw, Robert Southerland, William Spaniel, Robb Webb, George Zisiadis, and the many people who sat down with me in Rwanda. Also, my thanks to the many others who provided research and reporting help, including Edward Kaplas, Payal Sampat, Giti Zahedzadeh, and the wonderful folks at Skydive Elsinore.

A special thanks to the folks who made the data analysis possible: Chris Callahan at DDB Worldwide for being so patient with all my requests, and Stephen Goggin for actually wrestling the data down to something manageable.

One of the first articles that I read after I began researching this book was Jeremy Adam Smith and Pamela Paxton's "America's Trust Fall," in *The Compassionate Instinct: The Science of Human Goodness,* and the essay went a long way to shape my thinking. And finally my deepest gratitude to the writers who came before me, including Yochai Benkler, Steven Johnson, Bruce Schneier, James Surowiecki, Michael McCullough, Paul Seabright, Frans de Waal, Patricia Churchland, Michael Tomasello, Tom Tyler, and Martin Nowak. I gleefully had a chance to interview some of you. In other cases, I only managed to read your books seven or eight times. Thank you for paving the way.

The State of Trust

How much trust is there in your state? I calculated state-by-state numbers using data from the advertising firm DDB Worldwide Communications Group. I list some of the main findings below. For the full results, please visit my website: ulrichboser.com. The data are the most recent available.

Hall of Honor
In some areas, people are far more trusting of others, and in Maine, almost 90 percent of people said that they have some sort of faith in strangers. The most trusting states include New Hampshire, Maine, Utah, Iowa, and Nebraska.

Hall of Shame
In some states, almost no one reported completely trusting strangers. The least trusting states include Tennessee, Mississippi, Alabama, South Carolina, and Nevada.

Do You Trust People of Another Race?
Some states, like New Mexico, show relatively high rates of trust across races. But that isn't the case everywhere, and the states with the least amount of trust for people of another race include Alabama, Nebraska, Mississippi, Arkansas, and Louisiana.

Trust in Others: The Gender Gap
Trust across the male-female divide is low, and nationally just 5 percent

of people said that they completely trust people of the opposite gender. The laggard states include Indiana, Alabama, Nevada, and Kansas.

Trusting the Tax Man

Trust in government is highest in the states that surround Washington, D.C., and Virginia and Maryland top out the list of states with the most trust in government. In other states, trust in government is much lower, and in Alabama, Colorado, Pennsylvania, and Wyoming, more than 30 percent of people said that they have no trust at all in government.

Is Walmart a Trusted Brand?

Large companies don't always inspire large amounts of trust. This appears to be particularly true in the West, and Nevada, Colorado, and New Mexico have the lowest levels of trust in big business.

Source: DDB Worldwide Communications Group 2008, 2009

Tool Kit for Policymakers

There is one audience that may need a special tool kit on how to improve our trust in others: policymakers. Below are some proposals to help the nation rebuild its faith in others — and reinvest in its sagging social capital.

Build up a grassroots sense of community. Economically, politically, and socially, we've become far too isolated, and today only a minority of elementary schools even teach civics education.

- Support housing initiatives that rebuild cities and town in ways that emphasize socially and economically diverse communities.
- Invest in community policing, drug courts, and other forms of procedural justice that provide citizens with a greater voice in the legal system.
- Expand successful community-building programs and double the number of AmeriCorps participants.
- Resolve the status of the nation's undocumented immigrants.

Create a more fair and just economy. Economic mobility is low. Inequality is on the rise. We need to do more to build the nation's middle class — and hold corporations accountable for their actions. In short, we need to create a trustworthy economic system. I adapted the following recommendations from a recent report by my colleagues at the Center for American Progress: "300 Million Engines of Growth: A Middle-Out Plan for Jobs, Business, and a Growing Economy."[1]

- Pass comprehensive personal income tax reform.
- Raise the minimum wage and index it to half the average wage.
- Enact corporate income tax reform.

- Stop the worst effects of high-frequency trading through a transactions tax.

Empower individuals through education. When it comes to reforming the nation's school systems, there are some straightforward solutions:

- Support schools that lengthen the school day.
- Reform school funding so that it's both more equitable and effective, and have school dollars follow children instead of programs.
- Make college more affordable through Pell Grants.
- Allow college students to gain credit for learning outside the classroom.[2]

Improve government performance. It's not enough to build the policies that support our trust in others. We also need to improve the trustworthiness of our governmental institutions. This includes:

- Requiring agencies to create performance and other return-on-investment indicators that allow the public to measure success.
- Supporting new technologies that engage the public, improve decision-making, and make government more open and transparent.[3]
- Encouraging the development of Social Impact Bonds, which allow agencies to invest in new approaches to social programs.[4]

Notes

Introduction

1. Piers Paul Read, *Alive: The Story of the Andes Survivors* (New York: Avon Books, 1974), 14.

2. Nando Parrado, *Miracle in the Andes: 72 Days on the Mountain and My Long Trek Home* (New York: Three Rivers Press, 2006), 12.

3. Read, *Alive*, 24.

4. Parrado, *Miracle in the Andes*, 53.

5. "Stranded: I've Come from a Plane That Crashed on the Mountains," *Independent Lens*, PBS, May 19, 2009, www.pbs.org/independentlens/stranded/film.html and www.zeitgeistfilms.com/films/stranded/stranded.presskit.pdf. The PBS website contains thoughtful descriptions of the film, including an interview with the filmmaker Gonzalo Arijón, that were particularly helpful to my thinking. I first came across this idea in Stephen Holden's review of the film (Stephen Holden, "When Survival Hinged on Team Spirit," *New York Times*, October 21, 2008), which also helped shape my thinking.

6. Parrado, *Miracle in the Andes*, 177.

7. Ibid., 91.

8. "Stranded: I've Come from a Plane That Crashed on the Mountains."

9. "Partisan Polarization Surges in Bush, Obama Years: Trends in American Values, 1987–2012," Pew Research Center for the People & the Press, June 4, 2012, last modified October 18, 2013, www.people-press.org/fi les/legacy-pdf/06-04-12%20Values%20Release.pdf.

10. "Hospitality Group 2011 Employee Engagement Poll," *Maritz Research*, accessed July 28, 2013, www.maritz.com/~/media/Files/MaritzDotCom/White%20Papers/Executive Summary_Research.pdf.

11. Jeremy Adam Smith and Pamela Paxton, "America's Trust Fall," *The Compassionate Instinct: The Science of Human Goodness,* eds. Dacher Keltner, Jeremy Adam Smith, and Jason Marsh (New York: W. W. Norton & Company, 2010). In this chapter, Paxton and Smith argue that our best hope for improving social trust is our innate sense of trust, a notion which influenced my thinking.

12. Joseph Henrich et al., "'Economic Man' in Cross-Cultural Perspective: Behavioral Experiments in 15 Small-Scale Societies," *Behavioral and Brain Sciences* 28, no. 6 (December 2005): 795–815. I interviewed Henrich, Professor in the Departments of Psychology and Economics at the University of British Columbia, in December 2012.

13. David G. Rand, Joshua D. Greene, and Martin A. Nowak, "Spontaneous Giving and Calculated Greed," *Nature* 489 (September 2012): 427–30. I interviewed Rand, assistant professor of psychology, economics, cognitive science, at the School of Management at Yale University, in February 2013.

14. See Eva Cox, as cited in "Review of the Social Capital Measurement Literature," February 2001, Community Service and Research Centre, University of Queensland, Ipswich, www.uq.edu.au/boilerhouse/goodna-sip/media/section8/soccap.pdf.

15. Yochai Benkler, *The Penguin and the Leviathan: How Cooperation Triumphs over Self-Interest* (New York: Crown Business, 2011); Bruce Schneier, *Liars and Outliers: Enabling the Trust That Society Needs to Thrive* (Indianapolis: John Wiley & Sons, 2012); Tom Tyler, *Why People Cooperate: The Role of Social Motivations* (Princeton, NJ: Princeton University Press, 2010). Also see Michael Tomasello, *Why We Cooperate* (Cambridge, MA: MIT Press, 2009); Nowak and Highfield, *SuperCooperators* (New York: Free Press, 2012); Patricia S. Churchland, *Braintrust: What Neuroscience Tells Us About Morality* (Princeton, NJ: Princeton University Press, 2011); and Paul Seabright, *The Company of Strangers: A Natural History of Economic Life* (Princeton, NJ: Princeton University Press, 2010). Also helpful and influential to my thinking, although less recent, are Fukuyama's *Trust* and Robert D. Putnam, *Bowling Alone: The Collapse and Revival of American Community* (New York: Simon & Schuster, 2000), and James Surowiecki, *The Wisdom of Crowds* (New York: First Anchor Books, 2004).

16. Jeremy Adam Smith and Pamela Paxton, "America's Trust Fall."

17. Denise M. Rousseau and others, "Not So Different After All: A Cross-Discipline View of Trust," *Academy of Management Review* 23, no. 3 (July 1998): 393–404.

18. Ibid.

19. "Congress Less Popular than Cockroaches, Traffic Jams," Public Policy Polling, January 8, 2013, www.publicpolicypolling.com/main/2013/01/congress-less-popular-than-cockroaches-traffic-jams.html.

Chapter 1

1. Donja Darai and Silvia Grätz, "*Golden Balls:* A Prisoner's Dilemma Experiment," working paper (University of Zurich Socioeconomic Institute, July 2010), accessed on September 13, 2013. There are a number of old episodes of the show available online. My personal favorite, "*Golden Balls.* The Weirdest Split or Steal Ever!," can be seen on YouTube, accessed on August 10, 2013, www.youtube.com/watch?v=SoqjK3TWZE8.

2. Over the years, there have been lots of imaginings of the Prisoner's Dilemma, and Split or Steal is essentially a one-shot dilemma. My favorite is James Gleick's creative description. See "Prisoner's Dilemma Has Unexpected Applications," *New York Times,* June 17, 1986, www.nytimes.com/1986/06/17/science/prisoner-s-dilemma-has-unexpected-applications.html. Also see descriptions of the Trust Game by Paul Zak and in Kay-Yut Chen and Marin Krakovsky, *Secrets of the Moneylab: How Behavioral Economics Can Improve Your Business* (New York: Portfolio, 2010).

3. Cristina Bicchieri, Erte Xiao, and Ryan Muldoon, "Trustworthiness Is a Social Norm, but Trusting Is Not," *Politics Philosophy Economics* 10, no. 2 (May 2011): 170–187. Also

see Colin F. Camerer, *Behavioral Game Theory: Experiments in Strategic Interaction* (Princeton, NJ: Princeton University Press, 2003).

4. See Paul Zak, *Moral Molecule: The Source of Love and Prosperity* (New York: Dutton, 2012). Zak told me that this series of Trust Game studies was done with college students.

5. L. Cameron and others, "Little Emperors: Behavioral Impacts of China's One-Child Policy," *Science* 339, no 6122 (February 2013): 953–957.

6. Solitary Confinement: Hearing Before the Judiciary Subcommittee on the Constitution, Civil Rights, and Human Rights, United States Senate, June 19, 2012, 112th Congress, statement of Craig Haney, professor of psychology, University of California, Santa Cruz, accessed on August 9, 2013, www.judiciary.senate.gov/pdf/12-6-19HaneyTestimony.pdf. Also see Atul Gawande, "Hellhole: The United States Holds Tens of Thousands of Inmates in Long-Term Solitary Confinement. Is This Torture?" *New Yorker,* March 30, 2009.

7. Michael S. Gazzaniga, *Human: The Science Behind What Makes Us Unique* (New York: HarperCollins, 2008).

8. R. A. Hill and P. C. Lee, "Predation Risk as an Influence on Group Size in Cercopithecoid Primates: Implications for Social Structure," *Journal of Zoology* 245 (1998): 447–456.

9. John T. Cacioppo and William Patrick, *Loneliness: Human Nature and the Need for Social Connection* (New York: W. W. Norton & Company, 2008).

10. Matthew Lieberman, *Social* (New York: Crown, 2013). Also see David Brooks, "What Data Can't Do," *New York Times,* last modified February 18, 2013, http://www.nytimes.com/2013/02/19/opinion/brooks-what-data-cant-do.html.

11. Brooks, "What Data Can't Do."

12. Jonathan Haidt, *The Righteous Mind: Why Good People Are Divided by Politics and Religion* (New York: Vintage Books, 2012), xxii.

13. Roderick M. Kramer, "Rethinking Trust," *Harvard Business Review,* June 2009, hbr.org/2009/06/rethinking-trust.

14. Robert Kurzban, "The Social Psychophysics of Cooperation: Nonverbal Communication in a Public Goods Game," *Journal of Nonverbal Behavior* 25, no. 4 (2001): 241–259.

15. My account of Stouffer's work relies on Joseph W. Ryan, "Samuel A. Stouffer and the American Soldier," *Journal of Historical Biography* 7 (Spring 2010): 100–137, and Leonard Wong and others, "U.S. Army War College, Why They Fight: Combat Motivation in the Iraq War," Strategic Studies Institute, July 1, 2003, www.strategicstudiesinstitute.army.mil/pubs/display.cfm?pubID=179. I first came across Stouffer's work in Sebastian Junger, *War* (New York: Hachette Book Group, 2010).

16. Ryan, "Samuel A. Stouffer and the American Soldier."

17. Wong, "U.S. Army War College."

18. For the summary of the effects of social connections, I relied on Bert N. Uchino, "Understanding the Links Between Social Support and Physical Health: A Life-Span Perspective with Emphasis on the Separability of Perceived and Received Support," *Perspectives on Psychological Science* 4, no. 3 (2009): 236–255. For the study on colds, see Sheldon Cohen and others, "Social Ties and Susceptibility to the Common Cold," *JAMA* 277, no. 24 (June 1997): 1940–1944. Also see George Vaillant, *Triumphs of Experience: The Men of the Harvard Grant Study* (Boston: Belknap Press, 2012).

19. Frans de Waal, *The Age of Empathy: Nature's Lessons for a Kinder Society* (New York: Broadway Books, 2010). I also interviewed de Waal in August 2012. Also see de Waal in Keltner, Smith, and Marsh, *The Compassionate Instinct*.

20. Robert H. Frank, *Passions Within Reason: The Strategic Role of the Emotions* (New York: W. W. Norton & Company, 1988). Also see Gazzaniga, *Human: The Science Behind What Makes Us Unique*, 131. Also see Robert H. Frank, "The Status of Moral Emotions in Consequentialist Moral Reasoning" (Free Enterprise: Values in Action Conference Series, 2005–2006).

21. Peter Singer, *The Expanding Circle: Ethics and Sociobiology* (New York: Farrar, Straus and Giroux, February 1981). I first came across Singer's work in Steven Pinker, *The Better Angels of Our Nature: Why Violence Has Declined* (New York: Penguin Books, 2011).

22. Peter Singer, *Writings on an Ethical Life* (New York: Ecco Press, 2000), xix.

23. Martin A. Nowak, "Why We Help: The Evolution of Cooperation," *Scientific American*, June 19, 2012. I also relied on Nowak and Highfield, *SuperCooperators*. I interviewed Nowak in May 2012.

24. Ibid.

25. Sue Carter, professor of psychiatry and the codirector of the Brain Body Center, interview, July 2012. I also relied on her writings for my account. See, for instance, C. Sue Carter and Lowell L. Getz, "Monogamy and the Prairie Vole," *Scientific American*, 1993. I first came across Carter's story in Steven Johnson, *Mind Wide Open: Your Brain and the Neuroscience of Everyday Life* (New York: Scribner, 2004). Also see Larry Young and Brian Alexander, *The Chemistry Between Us: Love, Sex, and the Science of Attraction* (New York: Current, 2012).

26. Steven Johnson, *Mind Wide Open*.

27. My account relies on interviews with Zak and his description of the event in *Moral Molecule*, 22.

28. Paul J. Zak and Stephen Knack, "Trust and Growth," *Economic Journal* 111, no. 470 (March 2001): 295–321.

29. Zak, *Moral Molecule*, 24.

30. Ibid., 13.

31. Adam Penenberg, "Social Networking Affects Brains Like Falling in Love," *Fast Company*, July/August 2010, www.fastcompany.com/1659062/social-networking-affects-brains-falling-love.

32. Michael Kosfeld and others, "Oxytocin Increases Trust in Humans," *Nature* 435 (June 2005): 673–676.

33. Adam Penenberg, "Social Networking Affects Brains Like Falling in Love." Also see Michael Haederle, "The Best Fiscal Stimulus: Trust," *Pacific Standard*, August 2010. Haederle also didn't report feeling all that much after a dose of the hormone. I visited Zak's lab in May 2012.

34. Paul Zak argues that empathy promotes oxytocin release. I vetted this idea with other researchers.

35. M. Nagasawa and others, "Dog's Gaze at Its Owner Increases Owner's Urinary Oxytocin During Social Interaction," *Hormones and Behavior* 55, no. 3 (2009): 434–441.

36. Patricia Churchland, *Braintrust*.

37. During the fact-checking process, de Dreu told me that "whether we can indeed call oxytocin a social glue is a bit oversimplifying (I may have done that, apologies). It would be better to say that oxytocin promotes social bonding with close others, including those seen as part of one's own group."

38. Adam J. Guastella, Philip B. Mitchell, and Mark R. Daddsa, "Oxytocin Increases Gaze to the Eye Region of Human Faces," *Biological Psychiatry* 63, no. 1 (January 2008): 3–5.

39. Gregor Domes and others, "Oxytocin Improves 'Mind-Reading' in Humans," *Biological Psychiatry* 61, no. 6 (March 2007): 731–733.

40. My account here relies on my interviews with Zak, and his account of the experiment in *Moral Molecule*. Also see Linda Geddes, "My Big Fat Nerd Wedding," *New Scientist* 205, no. 2747 (February 13, 2010): 32–35.

41. Jennifer A. Bartz and others, "Social Effects of Oxytocin in Humans: Context and Person Matter," *Trends in Cognitive Sciences* 15, no. 7 (2011): 301–309.

42. D. Scheele and others, "Oxytocin Modulates Social Distance Between Males and Females," *Journal of Neuroscience* 32, no. 46 (November 2012): 16074–16079.

43. Ed Yong, "One Molecule for Love, Morality, and Prosperity?" *Slate*, July 17, 2012.

44. Carsten K. W. de Dreu and others, "Oxytocin Promotes Human Ethnocentrism," *Proceedings of the National Academy of Sciences of the United States of America* 108, no. 4 (2011): 1262–1266. I interviewed de Dreu in July 2012. Yong also mentions de Dreu's study.

45. Michael Kosfeld, "Brain Trust," in *The Compassionate Instinct: The Science of Human Goodness,* eds. Dacher Keltner, Jeremy Adam Smith, and Jason Marsh (New York: W. W. Norton & Company, 2010).

Chapter 2

1. Stuart W. Sanders, *Perryville Under Fire: The Aftermath of Kentucky's Largest Civil War Battle* (Charleston, SC: History Press, 2012), 21.

2. St. John Richardson Liddell, *Liddell's Record* (Dayton, OH: Morningside House, 1985), 93.

3. My source for this account was John Fitch, *Annals of the Army of the Cumberland* (Philadelphia: J. B. Lippincott & Co, 1864). I first came across this story in Daniel N. Rolph, *My Brother's Keeper: Union and Confederate Soldiers' Acts of Mercy During the Civil War* (Mechanicsburg, PA: Stackpole Books, 2002). I also interviewed Rolph, historian and head of reference services at the Historical Society of Pennsylvania, in September 2012.

4. Duane Schultz, "Coming Together: Fredericksburg, 1862, for a Short Time, Soldiers Put Aside Their Weapons and Acted Like Friends," *News Tribune* (Tacoma, WA), December 9, 2012, www.thenewstribune.com/2012/12/09/2396239/coming-together-fredericksburg.html.

5. The detail about the *Nashville Dispatch* comes from James B. Jones Jr., *Tennessee in the Civil War: Selected Contemporary Accounts of Military and Other Events, Month by Month* (Jefferson, NC: McFarland & Company, 2011), 121.

6. Malcolm Brown and Shirley Seaton served as my source for my description of the

truces in the Napoleonic Wars, the Crimean War, and World War I. See "The Christmas Truce," BBC News, November 3, 1998, news.bbc.co.uk/2/hi/special_report/1998/10/98/world_war_i/197627.stm.

7. Robert Axelrod, *The Evolution of Cooperation* (New York: Basic Books, 1984).

8. Robert Axelrod, "Launching 'The Evolution of Cooperation,'" *Journal of Theoretical Biology* 299 (2012): 21–24.

9. For more on non-zero-sum games, see Axelrod, *Evolution of Cooperation,* and Robert Wright, *Nonzero: The Logic of Human Destiny* (New York: First Vintage Books, 2000).

10. Adam Cohen, *The Perfect Store: Inside eBay* (New York: Little, Brown and Company, 2002), 18. My request to interview Pierre Omidyar was declined.

11. Cohen, *The Perfect Store*, cites "a study by the Pew Research Center that year found that just 8 percent of Americans felt comfortable using a credit card online," 26. And if you can't recall the Internet circa 1995, take a look at this: Chris Higgins, "What the Internet Looked Like in 1995," Mental Floss, last modified March 26, 2013, mentalfloss.com/article/49676/what-internet-looked-1995.

12. "Spawning e-trepreneurs," CNN Money, February 18, 1999, money.cnn.com/1999/02/18/fortune/fortune_ebay.

13. Cohen, *The Perfect Store,* 351.

14. Ibid.

15. Ibid.

16. Ibid., 27.

17. Ibid., 26.

18. "The Feedback Forum with Pierre Omidyar," OnInnovation, last modified March 2008, www.oninnovation.com/videos/detail.aspx?video=1268&title=The%20Feedback%20Forum.

19. Nowak and Highfield, *SuperCooperators,* 52–53.

20. Ibid.

21. Donald W. Pfaff, *The Neuroscience of Fair Play: Why We (Usually) Follow the Golden Rule* (New York: Dana Press, 2007), 10.

22. Nowak and Highfield, *SuperCooperators.*

23. "The Feedback Forum with Pierre Omidyar."

24. For the idea of using Charlie Brown to highlight game theory, I am indebted to Avinash K. Dixit and Barry J. Nalebuff, *The Art of Strategy: A Game Theorist's Guide to Success in Business and Life* (New York: W. W. Norton & Company, 2008). Also see Presh Talwalkar, "Charlie Brown and Game Theory," Mind Your Decisions, accessed on August 12, 2013, mindyourdecisions.com/blog/2009/11/24/charlie-brown-and-game-theory/#.Ud3WYUHvvzg.

25. Robert Frank and Ben Bernanke, *Principles of Microeconomics* (New York: McGraw-Hill/Irwin, 2008), define a commitment problem as "a situation in which people cannot achieve their goals because of an inability to make credible threats or promises," 267. Also see "Commitment Problems," Game Theory 101, accessed on October 10, 2013, gametheory101.com/Commitment_Problems.html.

26. "Commitment Problems and Devices," Experimental Economics Center, Andrew

Young School of Policy Studies at Georgia State University, accessed on August 12, 2013, www.econport.org/content/teaching/modules/NFG/Commit.html.

27. Al Kamen, "Punching Their Tickets," *Washington Post,* May 12, 1997, appears to have come up with the term *Great New York City Parking War.* My account of this so-called war relies on Raymond Fisman and Edward Miguel, "Cultures of Corruption: Evidence from Diplomatic Parking Tickets," Working Paper no. 12312 (National Bureau of Economic Research, June 2006), accessed on September 13, 2013, www.nber.org/papers/w12312, as well as other news accounts.

28. John Goldman, "Powell Brokers Parking Peace," *Los Angeles Times,* August 10, 2002, articles.latimes.com/2002/aug/10/nation/na-parking10.

29. Fisman and Miguel, "Cultures of Corruption: Evidence from Diplomatic Parking Tickets."

30. Raymond Fisman, "Reforming Tony Soprano's Morals," *Forbes,* May 6, 2006, www.forbes.com/forbes/2006/0522/040.html.

31. Rand, Greene, and Nowak, "Spontaneous Giving and Calculated Greed."

32. Kahneman, *Thinking, Fast and Slow* (New York: Farrar, Straus and Giroux, 2011).

33. Schneier, *Liars and Outliers,* gives one of the best summaries of how societies induce cooperation, though Schneier doesn't spend much time on the notion of reciprocity or indirect reciprocity.

34. Ken Lee, "Why Is Paris Hilton Still Driving?," *People,* May 9, 2007, www.people.com/people/article/0,,20038364,00.html. Also see TMZ Staff, "Exclusive: Paris Busted for DUI," TMZ, September 7, 2006, www.tmz.com/2006/09/07/exclusive-paris-busted-for-dui.

35. Cal Fussman, "Paris Hilton: What I've Learned," *Esquire,* December 17, 2008, www.esquire.com/features/what-ive-learned/paris-hilton-quotes-0109.

36. I came across Ramirez's story in Jordan Ellenberg, "You Can't Trust Airport Security," *Wall Street Journal* (September 2, 2012). I interviewed Hector Ramirez in April 2013. I also relied on Tina Redine, "Subway Operator Recalls 9/11 Cortlandt Street Stop Rescue," NY1, September 10, 2011. Also see Harvey Molotch, *Against Security* (New York: Wiley, 2012).

Chapter 3

1. For information on the Rockefeller case, I relied on Mark Seal, *The Man in the Rockefeller Suit: The Astonishing Rise and Spectacular Fall of a Serial Impostor* (New York: Penguin Group, 2011), Kindle edition. Also helpful were Mark Seal, "The Man in the Rockefeller Suit," *Vanity Fair,* January 2009, and *Commonwealth v. Gerhartsreiter,* Case No. 10-P-1899, available at http://www.courthousenews.com/AppellateOpinions/10P1899.doc. I also consulted news articles and interviewed Seal in October 2012. I spoke to Rockefeller's lawyer, Brad Bailey, who told me that he had advised Rockefeller not to speak to the media. I also sent a letter to Clark Rockefeller. He did not respond.

2. Seal, *The Man in the Rockefeller Suit,* 2516. Also see Walter Kirn, "Pedigree," *New Yorker,* June 10, 2013.

3. Jonathan Saltzman and Andrew Ryan, "'Rockefeller' Said He Had New Wife," *Boston Globe,* May 29, 2009, www.boston.com/news/local/massachusetts/articles/2009/05/

29/rockefeller_claimed_he_had_new_wife_social_worker_testifies/?page=full. Also see David Schoetz, "Amber Alert Off, Little Girl Still Missing," ABC News, July 28, 2008, abcnews.go.com/US/story?id=5462371&page=2.

4. Seal, *The Man in the Rockefeller Suit,* 780.

5. Ibid., 3690.

6. Ibid., 3605. Also see Jonathan Saltzman and Andrew Ryan, "Ex-Wife Testifies She Was Fooled," *Boston Globe,* June 3, 2009, www.boston.com/news/local/massachusetts/articles/2009/06/03/rockefeller_ex_wife_testifies_she_was_fooled.

7. Ibid., 2099.

8. Ibid., 3551.

9. Ibid., 996.

10. Ibid., 4919.

11. Schoetz, "Amber Alert Off, Little Girl Still Missing."

12. Ben Waber made this point to me. Also see Ben Waber, *People Analytics: How Social Sensing Technology Will Transform Business and What It Tells Us About the Future of Work* (Upper Saddle River, NJ: FT Press, 2013).

13. "David Rockefeller, Sr.," *Forbes,* last modified March 2013, www.forbes.com/profile/david-rockefeller-sr.

14. Seal, *The Man in the Rockefeller Suit,* 2198.

15. Ibid.

16. Ibid., 2151.

17. Ibid.

18. For my account of the Clue party, I relied on ibid.

19. Ibid.

20. Ibid.

21. Alex Pentland, *Honest Signals: How They Shape Our World* (Cambridge, MA: MIT Press, 2008). Also see Alex Pentland, interview by Jennifer Robison, *Gallup Business Journal,* November 13, 2008, businessjournal.gallup.com/content/111766/news-flash-workplace-socializing-productive.aspx.

22. *Watergate: A Brief History with Documents,* ed. Stanley I. Kutler (Hoboken, NJ: Blackwell Publishing, 2010). I first came across the idea that conversations are often opaque in Daniel Menaker, *A Good Talk: The Story and Skill of Conversation* (New York: Twelve, 2010).

23. Waber, *People Analytics,* 14.

24. Saltzman and Ryan, "Ex-Wife Testifies She Was Fooled."

25. Clark Rockefeller, interview by Maria Cramer, John R. Ellement, and Michael Levenson, *Boston Globe,* August 24, 2008, www.boston.com/news/local/articles/2008/08/24/im_not_quite_sure_what_im_supposed_to_remember_i_dont_lose_much_thought_over_it.

26. Seal, *The Man in the Rockefeller Suit,* 3923.

27. Waber, *People Analytics,* 78–80.

28. Ibid., 105.

29. Ibid., 174.

30. *The Man in the Rockefeller Suit,* 4575–4577.

31. Ibid.

32. Portions of the text in this section first appeared in Ulrich Boser, "We're All Lying Liars: Why People Tell Lies, and Why White Lies Can Be OK," *U.S. News and World Report,* May 18, 2009, health.usnews.com/health-news/family-health/brain-and-behavior/articles/2009/05/18/were-all-lying-liars-why-people-tell-lies-and-why-white-lies-can-be-ok.

33. Dan Ariely, *The Honest Truth About Dishonesty: How We Lie to Everyone — Especially Ourselves* (New York: HarperCollins, 2012), 27. I exchanged emails with Ariely, who gave me a taped interview.

34. D'Vera Cohn, Paul Taylor, Mark Hugo Lopez, Catherine A. Gallagher, Kim Parker, and Kevin T. Maass, "Gun Homicide Rate Down 49% Since 1993 Peak; Public Unaware," *Pew Research Social & Demographic Trends,* May 7, 2013, www.pewsocialtrends.org/2013/05/07/gun-homicide-rate-down-49-since-1993-peak-public-unaware/.

35. "Uncut: FBI Video of Clark Rockefeller Interview," WCVBtv, YouTube, last modified June 9, 2009, www.youtube.com/watch?v=k4AomWp8dIA.

Chapter 4

1. I interviewed Semugabo in May 2013. I also paid Semugabo fifty dollars to cover his transportation costs for my interview with him and for his follow-up interviews with my researcher.

2. For background on the genocide, I relied on a number of sources, including "Leave None to Tell the Story: Genocide in Rwanda," Human Rights Watch, March 1, 1999, www.hrw.org/reports/1999/03/01/leave-none-tell-story, and Philip Gourevitch, *We Wish to Inform You that Tomorrow We Will Be Killed with Our Families: Stories from Rwanda* (New York: Picador, 1998).

3. Jean Hatzfeld, *Machete Season: The Killers in Rwanda Speak* (New York: Farrar, Straus and Giroux, 2003), 21.

4. "Relationships/Sex: Advice for Cheaters and Their Partners," *Dr. Phil,* accessed on September 11, 2013, www.drphil.com/articles/article/127.

5. "Bud Welch (USA)," *The Forgiveness Project,* March 29, 2010, theforgivenessproject.com/stories/bud-welch-usa. I first came across Welch's story in Michael McCullough, *Beyond Revenge: The Evolution of the Forgiveness Instinct* (San Francisco: Jossey-Bass, 2008).

6. Paul Tullis, "Can Forgiveness Play a Role in Criminal Justice?," *New York Times,* January 4, 2013, www.nytimes.com/2013/01/06/magazine/can-forgiveness-play-a-role-in-criminal-justice.html?pagewanted=all.

7. McCullough, *Beyond Revenge,* 14.

8. This is widely cited. I first came across the idea in Amy Sullivan, "Rwanda's 'Miracle' of Forgiveness," *USA Today,* February 15, 2010, usatoday30.usatoday.com/NEWS/usaedition/2010-02-15-column15_ST_U.htm.

9. The soap opera has been widely covered. I first came across it in Michael Kavanagh, "Love in the Time of Reconciliation," On the Media, July 6, 2007, http://www.onthemedia.org/story/129500-love-in-the-time-of-reconciliation/.

10. Pete Rose and Rick Hill, *My Prison Without Bars* (Emmaus, PA: Rodale Press,

2000), 320. I first came across Rose's story in Rick Hampson, "Can You Forgive Lance Armstrong?," *USA Today,* January 18, 2013, www.usatoday.com/story/news/nation/2013/01/17/forgive-lance-armstrong-redemption/1843073.

11. I interviewed Ervin Staub, professor of psychology emeritus at the University of Massachusetts, Amherst, in December 2012. Also see Ervin Staub, *The Psychology of Good and Evil: Why Children, Adults, and Groups Help and Harm Others* (Cambridge, UK: Cambridge University Press, 2003).

12. Elizabeth Paluck, "Reducing Intergroup Prejudice and Conflict Using the Media: A Field Experiment in Rwanda," *Journal of Personality and Social Psychology* 96, no. 3 (March 2009): 574–587.

13. As cited in Gregory H. Stanton, *Journal of Genocide Research* 6, no. 2 (June 2004): 211–228.

14. "Frequently Asked Questions About Venomous Snakes," Department of Wildlife Ecology and Conservation at the University of Florida, accessed on September 11, 2013, ufwildlife.ifas.ufl.edu/venomous_snake_faqs.shtml.

15. "Shark Attack Statistics," Oceana, oceana.org/en/our-work/protect-marine-wildlife/sharks/learn-act/shark-attack-statistics.

16. Amanda Ripley, *The Unthinkable: Who Survives When Disaster Strikes — and Why* (New York: Three Rivers Press, 2008), 33. Also see David Ropeik and George Gray, *Risk: A Practical Guide for Deciding What's Really Safe and What's Really Dangerous in the World Around You* (New York: Houghton Mifflin Company, 2002), Barry Glassner, *Culture of Fear: Why Americans Are Afraid of the Wrong Things* (New York: Perseus, 2010), and Bruce Schneier, "The Psychology of Security," Schneier on Security, accessed on September 11, 2013, www.schneier.com/essay-155.html#sdendnote29anc.

17. Ropeik and Gray, *Risk,* 2.

18. Elie Wiesel, *Night,* trans. Marion Wiesel (New York: Hill and Wang, 1972).

19. My account of Wiesel's investment in the Madoff scheme — including Wiesel's quotes — comes from "The Madoff Panel Transcript," *Upstart Business Journal,* February 26, 2009, upstart.bizjournals.com/executives/2009/02/26/Wiesel-and-Madoff-Transcript.html?page=all.

20. Tina Rosenberg, *Join the Club: How Peer Pressure Can Transform the World* (New York: W. W. Norton, 2011).

21. Andrew Howard, "Groupthink and Corporate Governance Reform: Changing the Formal and Informal Decisionmaking Processes of Corporate Boards," *Southern California Interdisciplinary Law Journal* 20, no. 2 (January 2011): 425–456.

22. G. S. Berns et al., "Neurobiological Correlates of Social Conformity and Independence During Mental Rotation," *Biological Psychiatry* 58, no. 3 (August 2005): 245–253. Also see Sandra Blakeslee, "What Other People Say May Change What You See," *New York Times,* June 28, 2005, www.nytimes.com/2005/06/28/science/28brai.html.

23. Berns, "Neurobiological Correlates of Social Conformity and Independence During Mental Rotation."

24. Blakeslee, "What Other People Say May Change What You See."

25. Paul Rusesabagina, Tom Zoellner, *An Ordinary Man: An Autobiography* (New York: Penguin, 2007).

26. My account of Tajfel's life relies on the work of Peter Robinson, *Social Groups and Identities: Developing the Legacy of Henri Tajfel* (Oxford: Butterworth-Heinemann, 1996), and Henri Tajfel, *Human Groups and Social Categories: Studies in Social Psychology* (Cambridge, UK: Cambridge University Press, 1981).

27. Henri Tajfel, "Experiments in Intergroup Discrimination," *Scientific American* 223 (1970): 96–102.

28. Jeremy N. Bailenson and others, "Facial Similarity Between Voters and Candidates Causes Influence," *Public Opinion Quarterly* 72, no. 5 (2008): 935–961.

29. Christie Nicholson, "How We Fool Ourselves Over and Over," *Scientific American,* June 19, 2010, www.scientificamerican.com/podcast/episode.cfm?id=how-we-fool-ourselves-over-and-over-10-06-19.

30. Stanley Milgram, "Some Conditions of Obedience and Disobedience to Authority," *Human Relations* 18, no. 1 (February 1965): 57–76.

31. "Justice Compromised: The Legacy of Rwanda's Community-Based Gacaca Courts," Human Rights Watch, 2011, www.hrw.org/sites/default/files/reports/rwanda0511webw cover_0.pdf.

32. "How Rwanda Judged Its Genocide," *Africa Research Institute,* April 2012, www .africaresearchinstitute.org/files/counterpoints/docs/How-Rwanda-judged-its-genocide-E6QODPW0KV.pdf.

33. Ibid.

34. Chuck Korr and Marvin Close, *More Than Just a Game: Soccer vs. Apartheid: The Most Important Soccer Story Ever Told* (New York: Thomas Dunne Books, 2008).

35. Lynne Duke, "Apartheid-Era Jail Restored as a Monument," *Washington Post,* January 27, 1997, www.washingtonpost.com/wp-srv/inatl/africa/jan/31/sajail.htm.

36. Jeré Longman, "Origins of Tournament in an Infamous Prison," *New York Times,* July 5, 2010, www.nytimes.com/2010/07/06/sports/soccer/06robben.html?pagewanted=all& _r=0.

37. Korr and Close, *More Than Just a Game,* 27.

38. Marcy R. Podkopacz, Deborah A. Eckberg, and Keri Zehm, "Drug Court Defendant Experience and Fairness Study," Fourth Judicial District of the State of Minnesota (June 2004), www.mncourts.gov/Documents/4/Public/Research/Drug_Court_Fairness_Report %282004%29.pdf.

39. I interviewed Fredrik Kazigwemo in May 2013. I donated fifty dollars to the Reconciliation Village at the request of one of the village's staff.

40. Zack Baddorf, "Reconciliation Village Hosts Victims, Perpetrators of Rwandan Genocide," Voice of America, September 17, 2010,www.voanews.com/content/reconciliation-village-hosts-victims-prepetrators-of-rwandan-genocide-103207594/155845.html.

41. Peter H. Kim and others, "Removing the Shadow of Suspicion: The Effects of Apology Versus Denial for Repairing Competence- Versus Integrity-Based Trust Violations," *Journal of Applied Psychology* 89, no. 1 (February 2004): 104–118. I also interviewed Kim, associate professor of management and organization at the USC Marshall School of Business, in December 2012.

42. Carol Dweck, *Mindset: The New Psychology of Success* (New York: Ballantine Books, 2008). Also see "Brainology: Transforming Students' Motivation to Learn," *Indepen-*

dent School Magazine, Winter 2008, www.nais.org/Magazines-Newsletters/ISMagazine/Pages/Brainology.aspx.

43. Dweck, *Mindset,* 152.

44. J. A., "Speed Is Not Everything," *Economist,* January 2, 2013, www.economist.com/blogs/theworldin2013/2013/01/fastest-growing-economies-2013.

45. Marc Sommers, "The Darling Dictator of the Day," *New York Times,* May 27, 2012, www.nytimes.com/2012/05/28/opinion/Paul-Kagame-The-Darling-Dictator-of-the-day.html.

46. "Former President Clinton Announces Winners of the Third Annual Clinton Global Citizen Awards," Clinton Global Initiative, September 23, 2009, press.clintonglobal initiative.org/press_releases/former-president-clinton-announces-winners-of-the-third-annual-clinton-global-citizen-awards.

47. Jeffrey Gettleman, "Rwanda Pursues Dissenters and the Homeless," *New York Times,* April 30, 2010, www.nytimes.com/2010/05/01/world/africa/01rwanda.html.

48. Jean Hatzfeld, *Machete Season: The Killers in Rwanda Speak* (New York: Farrar, Straus and Giroux, 2003), 83.

49. Dietlind Stolle, Stuart Soroka, and Richard Johnston, "When Does Diversity Erode Trust? Neighborhood Diversity, Interpersonal Trust and the Mediating Effect of Social Interactions," *Political Studies* 56, no. 1 (March 2008): 57–75.

50. Bruno Frey, "Crowding Out and Crowding In of Intrinsic Preferences," in *Reflexive Governance for Global Public Goods,* eds. Eric Brousseau, Tom Dedeurwaerdere, and Bernd Siebenhüner (Cambridge, MA: MIT Press, 2012).

Chapter 5

1. My account of the first football game relies on two sources: "Rutgers 6 Princeton 4 College Field, New Brunswick, NJ," *Scarlet Knights,* accessed on September 11, 2013, scarletknights.com/football/history/first-game.asp, and Allen Barra, "The First Down, Ever," *Wall Street Journal,* November 7, 2009, online.wsj.com/article/SB10001424052748 703932904574511921170497590.html.

2. "In His Own Words: Quotes by Lombardi," ESPN Classic, accessed on September 11, 2013, espn.go.com/classic/quotes_Lombardi.html.

3. Bill Walsh, Steve Jamison, and Craig Walsh, *The Score Takes Care of Itself: My Philosophy of Leadership* (New York: Portfolio Trade, 2010), 85.

4. Paul Zimmerman, "Revolutionaries," *Sports Illustrated,* August 17, 1998, sports illustrated.cnn.com/vault/article/magazine/MAG1013561/5/index.htm.

5. My account relies on Gary Myers, *The Catch: One Play, Two Dynasties, and the Game That Changed the NFL* (New York: Three Rivers Press, 2009), and David Harris, *The Genius: How Bill Walsh Reinvented Football and Created an NFL Dynasty* (New York: Random House, 2008). Also see video footage of the game online: "49ers: Remember the Catch (Montana to Dwight Clark)," YouTube, May 24, 2012, www.youtube.com/watch?v=zBHjtcr7wQM.

6. Putnam, *Bowling Alone: The Collapse and Revival of American Community.*

7. Walsh, Jamison, and Walsh, *The Score Takes Care of Itself,* 28.

8. Ibid., 131.

9. Ibid., 113.

10. Harris, *The Genius*, 81.

11. This anecdote comes from Walsh, Jamison, and Walsh, *The Score Takes Care of Itself,* 34.

12. Harris, *The Genius*, 91.

13. Walsh, Jamison, and Walsh, *The Score Takes Care of Itself,* 112.

14. Ibid.

15. David Schkade, Cass R. Sunstein, and Reid Hastie, "What Happened on Deliberation Day?," Working Paper no. 298 (University of Chicago Law and Economics, June 2006), accessed on September 13, 2013, www.law.uchicago.edu/files/files/298.pdf.

16. Surowiecki, *The Wisdom of Crowds.*

17. Bill Walsh, interview by Richard Rapaport, *Harvard Business Review,* January 1993, hbr.org/1993/01/to-build-a-winning-team-an-interview-with-head-coach-bill-walsh/ar/4.

18. Walsh, Jamison, and Walsh, *The Score Takes Care of Itself,* 114.

19. Ibid., 48.

20. Ibid.

21. Ibid., 23.

22. Harris, *The Genius*, 82.

23. Walsh, Jamison, and Walsh, *The Score Takes Care of Itself,* 113.

24. Ibid., 23.

25. Michael W. Kraus, Cassy Huang, and Dacher Keltner, "Tactile Communication, Cooperation, and Performance: An Ethological Study of the NBA," *Emotion* 10, no. 5 (October 2010): 745–749. I interviewed Kraus, assistant professor of psychology at the University of Illinois, Urbana-Champaign, in May 2013. Also see Stephanie Pappas, "Touchy-Feely NBA Teams More Likely to Win," Livescience, November 9, 2010, www.livescience.com/11091-touchy-feely-nba-teams-win.html.

26. "Hall of Famers: Steve Young," Pro Football Hall of Fame, August 7, 2005, www.profootballhof.com/hof/member.aspx?PlayerId=252&tab=Speech.

Chapter 6

1. My account of the Ray Young incident relies on news articles that ran in the *Washington Post,* including Dan Morse, "Montgomery Man Gets 9 Years in Stabbing at Post Office," *Washington Post,* May 13, 2013, articles.washingtonpost.com/2013-05-13/local/39223226_1_ray-young-post-office-victim; Michael Laris, "Montgomery County Post Office Stabbing Suspect Charged with Attempted Murder," *Washington Post,* July 27, 2012, www.washingtonpost.com/blogs/crime-scene/post/montgomery-county-post-office-stabbing-suspect-charged-with-attempted-murder/2012/07/27/gJQAg1gnDX_blog.html; and Michael Laris, "Man Held in Stabbing at Md. Post Office," *Washington Post,* July 27, 2012, articles.washingtonpost.com/2012-07-27/local/35488756_1_postal-worker-life-threatening-injuries-baseball-bat. I contacted Ray Young's lawyer, Gary Courtois, in December 2012. I did not receive a reply. I first came across the idea of queue rage in Seth Stevenson, "What You Hate Most About Waiting in Line," *Slate,* June 1, 2012.

2. Jerome Taylor, "Couple Found Guilty of Death in Supermarket Queue," *Independent*

(London), February 27, 2009, www.independent.co.uk/news/uk/crime/couple-found-guilty-of-death-in-supermarket-queue-1633408.html.

3. David Hunt, "Post Office Line Rage Sends Jacksonville Man over the Edge," *Jax Air News* (Jacksonville, FL), July 1, 2011, jaxairnews.jacksonville.com/news/crime/2011-07-01/story/post-office-line-rage-sends-jacksonville-man-over-edge.

4. "Express-Lane Dispute Costs Shopper Part of Her Nose," Associated Press, April 11, 1998.

5. Alex Stone, "Why Waiting Is Torture," *New York Times,* August 18, 2012. I also interviewed Richard Larson, Mitsui Professor of Engineering Systems at MIT, in December 2012.

6. Anat Rafaeli and others, "Queues and Fairness: A Multiple Study Experimental Investigation," Technical Report (Faculty of Industrial Engineering and Management at the Technion-Israel Institute of Technology), ie.technion.ac.il/Home/Users/anatr/JAP-Fairness-Submission.pdf. I first came across this study in Stone, "Why Waiting Is Torture."

7. Bruno Wicker and others, "Both of Us Disgusted in My Insula: The Common Neural Basis of Seeing and Feeling Disgust," *Neuron* 40, no. 3 (October 2003): 655–664.

8. Golnaz Tabibnia, Ajay B. Satpute, and Matthew D. Lieberman, "The Sunny Side of Fairness: Preference for Fairness Activates Reward Circuitry (and Disregarding Unfairness Activates Self-Control Circuitry)," *Psychological Science* 19, no. 4 (April 2008): 339–347. Also see Wray Herbert, *On Second Thought: Outsmarting Your Mind's Hard-Wired Habits* (New York: Broadway Books, 2010).

9. Paul Woodruff, *The Ajax Dilemma: Justice, Fairness, and Rewards* (Oxford: Oxford University Press, 2011). I interviewed Paul Woodruff, Mary Helen Thompson Professor of the Humanities at the University of Texas in Austin, in January 2013. I first came across the book in an excellent review, Josh Rothman, "Paul Woodruff's 'The Ajax Dilemma,'" *Boston Globe,* October 26, 2011, and that article also helped shape my thinking.

10. Ovid, *Metamorphoses,* trans. Rolfe Humphries (Bloomington: Indiana University Press), 318.

11. Sophocles, *Ajax,* trans. R. C. Trevelyan, classics.mit.edu/Sophocles/ajax.html.

12. Michael I. Norton and Dan Ariely, "Building a Better America — One Wealth Quintile at a Time," *Perspectives on Psychological Science* 6, no. 1 (January 2011): 9–12. I interviewed Norton, associate professor of business administration at the Harvard Business School, in January 2012.

13. Raj Chetty and others, "Mobility in the 100 Largest Commuting Zones," Equality of Opportunity Project, accessed on September 16, 2013, www.equality-of-opportunity.org/index.php/city-rankings/city-rankings-100.

14. Tom Hertz, "Understanding Mobility in America," Center for American Progress, April 26, 2006, www.americanprogress.org/issues/economy/news/2006/04/26/1917/understanding-mobility-in-america.

15. Richard Florida, "The High Inequality of U.S. Metro Areas Compared to Countries," *Atlantic Cities,* October 9, 2012, www.theatlanticcities.com/jobs-and-economy/2012/10/high-inequality-us-metro-areas-compared-countries/3079.

16. Eric M. Uslaner, "Middle Class Series: Income Inequality in the United States Fuels Pessimism and Threatens Social Cohesion," Center for American Progress, December 5, 2012, www.americanprogress.org/issues/economy/report/2012/12/05/46871/income-inequality-in-the-united-states-fuels-pessimism-and-threatens-social-cohesion.

Chapter 7

1. For my description of Somalia, I relied on James Fergusson, *The World's Most Dangerous Place: Inside the Outlaw State of Somalia* (Boston: Da Capo Press, 2013); Mary Jane Harper, *Getting Somalia Wrong? Faith, War and Hope in a Shattered State* (New York: Zed Books, 2012); and "Somalia," CIA World Factbook, last modified August 22, 2013, www.cia.gov/library/publications/the-world-factbook/geos/so.html. Also helpful was Tim Harford, "The Economics of Trust," *Forbes,* July 20, 2010.

2. My account of Mohamed Aden Guled relies on William Finnegan, "Letter from Mogadishu," *New Yorker,* March 20, 1995, www.newyorker.com/archive/1995/03/20/1995_03_20_064_TNY_CARDS_000368240.

3. "Living in Somalia's Anarchy," BBC, November 18, 2004, news.bbc.co.uk/2/hi/4017147.stm.

4. Abdi Guled, "A New, Dangerous Job in Mogadishu: Tax Collector," Associated Press, July 29, 2013, bigstory.ap.org/article/new-dangerous-job-mogadishu-tax-collector.

5. Onora O'Neill, "Lecture 1: Without Trust We Cannot Stand," BBC Radio 4, last modified April 2004, www.bbc.co.uk/radio4/reith2002/lecture1.shtml.

6. "Public Trust in Government: 1958–2013," Pew Research Center, last modified January 31, 2013, www.people-press.org/2013/01/31/trust-in-government-interactive.

7. Onora O'Neill, "Lecture 1: Without Trust We Cannot Stand," BCC Radio 4, last modified April 2004, http://www.bbc.co.uk/radio4/reith2002/lecture1.shtml.

8. Jan Delhey and Christian Welzel, "Generalizing Trust, How Outgroup-Trust Grows Beyond Ingroup-Trust," *World Values Research* 5, no. 3 (2012), www.worldvaluessurvey.org/wvs/articles/folder_published/paperseries_46/files/WVR_05_03_Delhey_and_Welzel.pdf.

9. My account of William Donald Schaefer's work relies on the following sources: "The Hero of Baltimore," *Baltimore Sun,* April 18, 2011, articles.baltimoresun.com/2011-04-18/news/bs-ed-schaefer-20110418_1_don-schaefer-comptroller-william-donald-schaefer; Adam Bernstein, "William Donald Schaefer Dies at 89; Maryland Governor, Baltimore Mayor Had Trademark Style," *Washington Post,* April 18, 2011, articles.washingtonpost.com/2011-04-18/local/35229892_1_baltimore-mayor-william-donald-schaefer-baltimore-aquarium; Doug Donovan, "William Donald Schaefer Leaves 'Do It Now' Legacy on Maryland Politics," *North Baltimore Patch,* April 20, 2011, northbaltimore.patch.com/groups/editors-picks/p/william-donald-schaefer-dies; Robert D. McFadden, "William Schaefer, Baltimore Mayor, Dies at 89," *New York Times,* April 18, 2011, www.nytimes.com/2011/04/19/us/19schaefer.html?pagewanted=all; and C. Fraser Smith, *William Donald Schaefer: A Political Biography* (Baltimore: Johns Hopkins University Press, 1999).

10. "William Donald Schaefer over the Years," *Baltimore Sun,* April 26, 2011, articles

.baltimoresun.com/2011-04-26/news/bs-md-schaefer-quotes-20110426_1_harborplace-william-donald-schaefer-mayor.

11. Bernstein, "William Donald Schaefer Dies at 89."

12. John Podesta and Reece Rushing, "Doing What Works: Building a Government That Delivers Greater Value and Results to the American People," Center for American Progress, February 18, 2010, www.americanprogress.org/issues/open-government/report/2010/02/18/7267/doing-what-works.

13. U.S. Government Accountability Office, *Opportunities to Reduce Potential Duplication in Government Programs, Save Tax Dollars, and Enhance Revenue*, GAO-11-318SP (Washington, D.C.: United States Government Printing Office, March 2011), www.gao.gov/new.items/d11318sp.pdf.

14. Ulrich Boser, "Return on Educational Investment: A District-by-District Evaluation of U.S. Educational Productivity," Center for American Progress, January 19, 2011, www.americanprogress.org/issues/education/report/2011/01/19/8902/return-on-educational-investment.

15. My account of Blair's government reform efforts relies on news sources as well as Michael Barber, *Instruction to Deliver: Fighting to Transform Britain's Public Services* (York, UK: Methuen, 2008). I interviewed Barber in March 2013.

16. David Bamber, "The Victims: 'A Lot of These Schemes Are Gimmicks,'" *Telegraph* (London), January 14, 2001.

17. Philip Johnston, "ID Cards Don't Work — Even Tony Says So," *Telegraph* (London), December 4, 2006, www.telegraph.co.uk/comment/personal-view/3634909/ID-cards-dont-work-even-Tony-says-so.html.

18. Barber, *Instruction to Deliver*, 273.

19. For the Hamilton quote, I relied on "The Federalist Papers: No. 70," Yale Law School, Lillian Goldman Law Library, accessed on September 25, 2013, avalon.law.yale.edu/18th_century/fed70.asp. I first came across Hamilton's idea in Larry Jay Diamond, "Three Paradoxes of Democracy," *Journal of Democracy* 1, no. 3 (Summer 1990): 48–60.

20. Dana R. Carney and others, "People with Power Are Better Liars" (unpublished, Columbia University, 2009), www.engaged-zen.org/PDFarchive/PowerLying.pdf.

21. "Madison Debates," Yale Law School, Lillian Goldman Law Library, accessed on November 26, 2013, avalon.law.yale.edu/18th_century/debates_711.asp.

22. I interviewed Ronald MacLean-Abaroa in January 2012. I also relied on Robert Klitgaard, Ronald MacLean-Abaroa, and H. Lindsey Parris, *Corrupt Cities: A Practical Guide to Cure and Prevention* (Oakland, CA: Institute for Contemporary Studies, 2000).

23. "The Paradox of Transparency," *Independent* (London), June 21, 2009, www.independent.co.uk/voices/editorials/leading-article-the-paradox-of-transparency-1711369.html.

24. Andrew J. Perrin and Sondra J. Smolek, "Who Trusts? Race, Gender, and the September 11 Rally Effect Among Young Adults," *Social Science Research* 38, no. 1 (March 2009): 134–145.

25. My account of Bud Clark relies on news accounts, including Gordon Oliver, "Mayor Bud's Wild Ride," *Oregonian* (Portland), December 13, 1992; Charles Hillinger, "Oregon:

A State Proud of Its Firsts: Women Hold Top Posts in Politics, Law Enforcement," *Los Angeles Times,* March 31, 1985, articles.latimes.com/1985-03-31/news/vw-19187_1_oregon-state-legislature; and Lauren Cowen, "Mayor Clark's Struggle to Be Just Bud," *Oregonian,* October 1, 1989. I interviewed Clark via email in September 2013.

26. John Schrag, "This Bud's for You," *Willamette Week,* March 9, 2005.

27. Eileen Pincus-Walker, "Portland's Mayor: Unusual Politician," *NewsHour,* November 26, 1984. Also see Hillinger, "Oregon: A State Proud."

28. Cowen, "Mayor Clark's Struggle to Be Just Bud."

29. Stuart Wasserman, "Help for Politician Pours in, a Dollar at a Time; Constituents Pitch In to Pay Campaign Debts for Their Mayor, Whom They Have Fondly Tagged 'The Budster,'" *Los Angeles Times,* January 27, 1992, articles.latimes.com/1992-01-27/news/mn-626_1_campaign-debts.

30. Steven Johnson, *Future Perfect: The Case for Progress in a Networked Age* (New York: Riverhead Trade, 2013).

31. Pamela Abramson, "Loose as a Goose in City Hall," *Newsweek,* March 25, 1985.

32. Barnes C. Ellis, "Bud Clark Gives Farewell Address Before City Club," *Oregonian* (Portland), December 12, 1992.

Chapter 8

1. John R. Hibbing and Elizabeth Theiss-Morse, *Congress as Public Enemy: Public Attitudes Toward American Political Institutions* (Cambridge, UK: Press Syndicate of the University of Cambridge, 1995). I interviewed Theiss-Morse, Willa Cather Professor of Political Science at the University of Nebraska–Lincoln, in January 2012.

2. Ezra Klein, "A Good Message Is Not Nearly as Important as a Fast Process," *Washington Post,* February 3, 2010, voices.washingtonpost.com/ezra-klein/2010/02/a_good_message_is_not_nearly_s.html. For polling data, see "Public Opinion on Health Care Issues," Henry J. Kaiser Family Foundation, March 2010, kaiserfamilyfoundation.files.wordpress.com/2013/01/8058-f.pdf.

3. John E. Mueller, *Capitalism, Democracy, and Ralph's Pretty Good Grocery* (Princeton, NJ: Princeton University Press, 1999), 137.

4. My account of Gingrich's 1978 run for Congress relies on Steven M. Gillon, *The Pact: Bill Clinton, Newt Gingrich, and the Rivalry That Defined a Generation* (Oxford: Oxford University Press, 2008).

5. Ibid.

6. Thomas E. Mann and Norman J. Ornstein, *It's Even Worse Than It Looks: How the American Constitutional System Collided with the New Politics of Extremism* (New York: Basic Books, 2012), 38.

7. The "definer of civilization" quote comes from "Gingrich's Doodles," *Slate,* December 8, 2011, www.slate.com/slideshows/news_and_politics/gingrichs-doodles.html. Also see Mann and Ornstein, *It's Even Worse Than It Looks,* for details on Gingrich's early days in office.

8. Gail Sheehy, "The Inner Quest of Newt Gingrich," *Vanity Fair,* September 1995, www.pbs.org/wgbh/pages/frontline/newt/vanityfair1.html.

9. "The Long March of Newt Gingrich: 1978 speech by Gingrich," *Frontline,* accessed on September 26, 2013, www.pbs.org/wgbh/pages/frontline/newt/newt78speech.html.

10. David Osborne, "The Swinging Days of Newt Gingrich," *Mother Jones,* November 1, 1984, www.motherjones.com/politics/1984/11/newt-gingrich-shining-knight-post-reagan-right.

11. Sheryl Gay Stolberg, "Gingrich Stuck to Caustic Path in Ethics Battles," *New York Times,* January 26, 2012.

12. "Reid Statement on Romney's False Claims of Bipartisanship," Harry Reid: United States Senator from Nevada, November 2, 2012, www.reid.senate.gov/newsroom/pr_110212_.cfm.

13. Mann and Ornstein make this point. Also see "Parliamentary Parties in a Presidential System," Jack Balkin, balkin.blogspot.com/2010/11/parliamentary-parties-in-presidential.html.

14. Lydia Saad, "Conservatives Remain the Largest Ideological Group in U.S.," Gallup Politics, January 12, 2012, www.gallup.com/poll/152021/Conservatives-Remain-Largest-Ideological-Group.aspx.

15. Mickey Edwards, "How to Turn Republicans and Democrats Into Americans," *Atlantic,* June 7, 2011, www.theatlantic.com/magazine/archive/2011/07/how-to-turn-republicans-and-democrats-into-americans/308521.

16. Writer Robert Costa made this argument in an interview. See Ezra Klein, "Why Boehner Doesn't Just Ditch the Hard Right," *Washington Post,* October 1, 2013, www.washingtonpost.com/blogs/wonkblog/wp/2013/10/01/why-boehner-doesnt-just-ditch-the-right.

17. Chris Moody, "Newt Gingrich on Drug Laws, Entitlements and Campaigning," Yahoo! News, November 28, 2011, news.yahoo.com/blogs/ticket/newt-gingrich-drug-laws-entitlements-campaigning-yahoo-news-152936251.html.

18. Brad Johnson, "Gingrich's Great Global Warming Flip-Flop: From Cap-and-Trade to Drill-Baby-Drill," CampusProgress, March 25, 2011, thinkprogress.org/climate/2011/03/25/174957/newt-climate-flip-flops.

19. Ben Armbruster, "Gingrich Changes His Position: 'Waterboarding Is, by Every Technical Rule, Not Torture,'" ThinkProgress, November 29, 2011, thinkprogress.org/security/2011/11/29/377907/gingrich-waterboarding-not-torture.

20. Lois Romano, "Newt Gingrich, Maverick on the Hill: The New Right's Abrasive Point Man Talks of Changing His Tone and Tactics," *Washington Post,* January 3, 1985.

21. Ann H. Harvey and others, "Monetary Favors and Their Influence on Neural Responses and Revealed Preference," *Journal of Neuroscience* 30 (July 2010): 9597–9602. I first came across the study in Ariely, *The Honest Truth About Dishonesty.*

22. The figures from Obama's and Romney's contributions come from Melanie Mason and Joseph Tanfani, "Obama, Romney Break Fundraising Records," *Los Angeles Times,* December 7, 2012, articles.latimes.com/2012/dec/07/nation/la-na-campaign-money-20121207.

23. Jay Costa, "What's the Cost of a Seat in Congress?" MapLight, March 10, 2013, maplight.org/content/73190.

24. Hillel Aron, "LAUSD School Board District 4 Election: Absentee Ballot Results Show Steve Zimmer Leading Kate," *LAWeekly*, March 5, 2013, blogs.laweekly.com/informer/2013/03/lausd_school_board_district_4.php.

25. Ryan Grim and Sabrina Siddiqui, "Call Time for Congress Shows How Fundraising Dominates Bleak Work Life," *Huffington Post*, January 9, 2013, www.huffingtonpost .com/2013/01/08/call-time-congressional-fundraising_n_2427291.html.

26. Alex Blumberg, "Senator by Day, Telemarketer by Night," Planet Money, NPR, March 30, 2012, www.npr.org/blogs/money/2012/03/30/149648666/senator-by-day-telemarketer-by-night. Also see Andrea Seabrook and Alex Blumberg, "Take the Money and Run for Office," This American Life, www.npr.org/blogs/money/2012/03/26/149390968/take-the-money-and-run-for-office.

27. Lee Drutman, "The Political 1% of the 1% in 2012," Sunlight Foundation, June 24, 2013, sunlightfoundation.com/blog/2013/06/24/1pct_of_the_1pct.

28. Mike Allen, "Sheldon Adelson: Inside the Mind of the Mega-donor," Politico, September 23, 2012.

29. Neil King Jr. and Patrick O'Connor, "Gingrich's Secret Weapon: Newt Inc.," *Wall Street Journal*, May 9, 2011. Also see Dan Eggen, "Gingrich Think Tank Collected Millions from Health-Care Industry," *Washington Post*, November 17, 2011.

30. Ibid.

31. Tracy Campbell, *Deliver the Vote: A History of Election Fraud, an American Political Tradition, 1742–2004* (New York: Carroll & Graf Publishers, 2005), 5.

32. "Lobbyists," United States Senate, accessed on September 29, 2013, www.senate.gov/legislative/common/briefing/Byrd_History_Lobbying.htm.

33. Marc J. Hetherington, *Why Trust Matters: Declining Political Trust and the Demise of American Liberalism* (Princeton, NJ: Princeton University Press, 2005), 1–2.

34. M. J. Stephey, "Bush's Major-League Mistake," *Time*, March 27, 2012. I first came across this anecdote in Hetherington, *Why Trust Matters*.

35. "George W. Bush 2000 Campaign Ad," YouTube, accessed on September 29, 2013, www.youtube.com/watch?v=6FxL242-z6I. I first came across this example in Hetherington, *Why Trust Matters*.

36. Hetherington, *Why Trust Matters*, 2.

37. "House GOP Plans Anti-Washington Push in August," Associated Press, August 5, 2013, www.politico.com/story/2013/08/house-republicans-recess-plan-95180.html#ixzz 2eiiEh2yo.

38. My account of the murders relies on news reports of the crime, including Andrew Wolfe, "Murder Details Reveal Planning, Bragging," *Telegraph* (Nashua, NH), January 6, 2010, www.nashuatelegraph.com/news/517488-196/cout-documents-in-cates-murder-released.html; Joseph G. Cote, "Glover: Spader 'Euphoric' After Killing," *Telegraph* (Nashua, NH), October 29, 2010, www.nashuatelegraph.com/mobile/893384-264/glover-spader-euphoric-after-killing.html; Joseph Cote, "Friends: 'Creepy Chris' Was a Dork," *Telegraph* (Nashua, NH), March 18, 2011, www.nashuatelegraph.com/news/912792-196/live-online-gribbles-friends-describe-the-person.html; and Kathryn Marchocki, "In Released Court Records, Spader's Past Offers Few Clues to Cates Mur-

der," *New Hampshire Union Leader* (Manchester, NH), July 29, 2013, www.newhampshire
.com/article/20130730/NEWS03/130739973/-1/newhampshire1405&template=newhamp
shire1407.

39. John Ellement, "Judge Sentences Spader to Life; Says He Belongs in a 'Cage,'" *Boston Globe,* November 9, 2010.

40. Wolfe, "Murder Details Reveal Planning, Bragging."

41. Ibid.

42. See Randolph Roth, *American Homicide* (Cambridge, MA: Belknap Press, 2009). Over the past few years, I have interviewed Roth a number of times via email, most recently in March 2013. I first came across Roth's work in a review by Jill Lepore, "Rap Sheet," *New Yorker,* November 9, 2009. Lepore's review helped shape my thinking, though she takes a far more skeptical approach to Roth's work than I do.

43. Lynne Tuohy, "Killer Tells of Slashing Mother, Daughter," Associated Press, March 24, 2011, www.telegram.com/article/20110324/NEWS/103240848/1052.

44. Steven Spader, "To Who It May Concern," July 13, 2010, www.nashuatelegraph.com/csp/cms/sites/Telegraph/dt.common.streams.StreamServer.cls?STREAMOID=1Q5QFL
KDem82TvLBKXZV_vM$Cc1SQJbwTXJnQ8DE2VU0OAnE5WzdpaN1_ModR09H4
Aw$6wU9GSUcqtd9hs3TFeZCnovq69IZViKeqDZhqNLziaXiKG0K_ms4C2keQ054&
CONTENTTYPE=application/pdf&CONTENTDISPOSITION=newspader.pdf.

Chapter 9

1. I interviewed Casey Fenton in September 2013. I first came across Fenton's story in Rachel Botsman and Roo Rogers, *What's Mine Is Yours: The Rise of Collaborative Consumption* (New York: HarperCollins, 2010), 176. My thinking was also influenced by Patricia Marx's wonderful article on Couchsurfing: "You're Welcome," *New Yorker,* April 16, 2012, www.newyorker.com/reporting/2012/04/16/120416fa_fact_marx?currentPage=all.

2. Debra Lauterbach and others, "Surfing a Web of Trust: Reputation and Reciprocity on CouchSurfing.com" (paper presented at the International Conference on Computational Science and Engineering, August 29–31, 2009). I first came across the study in Marx, "You're Welcome."

3. I first came across Bob Redmond in Jed Lipinski, "You're Not a Stranger When You Leave," *New York Times,* August 31, 2011, www.nytimes.com/2011/09/01/garden/nudists-open-their-homes-to-budget-minded-travelers.html?pagewanted=all. I interviewed Edward Chu and Redmond in November 2012.

4. Clifford Nass and Corina Yen, *The Man Who Lied to His Laptop: What We Can Learn About Ourselves from Our Machines* (New York: Current, 2010), 3. I interviewed Nass in September 2013.

5. Ibid., 6.

6. Adam L. Penenberg, "Digital Oxytocin: How Trust Keeps Facebook, Twitter Humming," *Fast Company,* July 18, 2011, www.fastcompany.com/1767125/digital-oxytocin-how-trust-keeps-facebook-twitter-humming. Also see Adam L. Penenberg, "Social Networking Affects Brains Like Falling in Love," *Fast Company,* July 1, 2010, www
.fastcompany.com/1659062/social-networking-affects-brains-falling-love.

7. Some of the language in this paragraph comes from Ulrich Boser, "Are Schools Getting a Big Enough Bang for Their Education Technology Buck?," Center for American Progress, June 14, 2013, www.americanprogress.org/issues/education/report/2013/06/14/66485/are-schools-getting-a-big-enough-bang-for-their-education-technology-buck.

8. For my account of Robert Morris, I relied on news reports as well as Katie Hafner and John Markoff, *Cyberpunk: Outlaws and Hackers on the Computer Frontier,* rev. ed. (New York: Touchstone, 1995).

9. John Markoff, "Student Testifies His Error Jammed Computer Network," *New York Times,* January 19, 1990.

10. Ibid.

11. "Networks," Computer Museum History Center, accessed on September 29, 2013, libai.math.ncu.edu.tw/bcc16/pool/stuff/CMHC_timeline/timeline/topics/networks.page.htm.

12. For details on Morris's conviction, see John Markoff, "Computer Intruder Is Put on Probation and Fined $10,000," *New York Times,* May 5, 1990, www.nytimes.com/1990/05/05/us/computer-intruder-is-put-on-probation-and-fined-10000.html. For the detail about a man receiving three years' probation for sex abuse a few years later, see "Child Abuser Gets 3 Years of Probation," *Baltimore Sun,* June 8, 1993, articles.baltimoresun.com/1993-06-08/news/1993159067_1_supervised-probation-suspended-sentence-sykesville-man.

Chapter 10

1. Jeff Wise, *Extreme Fear: The Science of Your Mind in Danger* (New York: Palgrave Macmillan, 2009).

2. Zak, *Moral Molecule,* 95.

3. Specifically, Baumgartner said, "Sometimes you have to go up really high to understand how small you really are." See John Tierney, "24 Miles, 4 Minutes and 834 M.P.H., All in One Jump," *New York Times,* October 14, 2012, www.nytimes.com/2012/10/15/us/felix-baumgartner-skydiving.html.

4. Robert Wright, "Signing Off," *Atlantic,* January 8, 2013, www.theatlantic.com/international/archive/2013/01/signing-off/266925.

5. Roderick M. Kramer, "Rethinking Trust."

6. Eric M. Uslaner, "Middle Class Series: Income Inequality in the United States Fuels Pessimism and Threatens Social Cohesion."

Tool Kit for Policymakers

1. Jennifer Erickson and Michael Ettlinger, eds., "300 Million Engines of Growth: A Middle-Out Plan for Jobs, Business, and a Growing Economy," Center for American Progress, June 13, 2013, www.americanprogress.org/issues/economy/report/2013/06/13/66204/300-million-engines-of-growth.

2. Rebecca Klein-Collins, Amy Sherman, and Louis Soares, "Degree Completion Beyond Institutional Borders," Center for American Progress, October 28, 2010, www

.americanprogress.org/issues/labor/report/2010/10/28/8567/degree-completion-beyond-institutional-borders.

3. Podesta and Rushing, "Doing What Works."

4. Jitinder Kohli, Douglas J. Besharov, and Kristina Costa, "Social Impact Bonds: What Are Social Impact Bonds?" Center for American Progress, March 22, 2012, www.american progress.org/issues/open-government/report/2012/03/22/11175/what-are-social-impact-bonds.